GIANT
MORE BASIC SKILLS™
K-1 WORKBOOK

Modern Publishing
A Division of Unisystems, Inc.
New York, New York 10022

Cover art by Michelle Hill
Illustrated by Arthur Friedman
Educational Consultant, Shereen Gertel Rutman, M.S.

TO THE PARENTS

Dear Parents,

As your child's first and most important teacher, you can encourage your child's love of learning by participating in educational activities at home. Working together on the activities in this workbook will help your child build confidence, learn to reason, and develop skills necessary for early childhood education.

The following are some suggestions to help make your time together both enjoyable and rewarding.

- Choose a time when you and your child are relaxed.

- Provide a writing utensil that your child is familiar with.

- Don't attempt to do too many pages at one time or expect that every page be completed. Move on if your child is frustrated or loses interest.

- Praise your child's efforts.

- Discuss each page. Help your child relate the concepts in this book to everyday experiences.

ESSENTIAL SKILLS

The repetitive activities within each chapter have been designed to help children learn to sort, separate, put together, and figure out—the organizational skills so necessary for learning and thinking.

CHAPTER 1 Handwriting Skills

Learning to control the small muscles of the hand (**fine motor skill development**) allows the child to make the precise movements necessary for forming letters, while activities such as **writing from left to right**, **tracing**, and **forming lines** help to refine **eye/hand coordination**. Making **associations**—recognizing what things "go together" (for example, a dog and a bone)—enables a child to recognize that an uppercase "A" and a lowercase "a" go together.

CHAPTER 2 Colors, Shapes, and Numbers

Looking at familiar shapes helps children notice similarities and differences. Activities in which the child reproduces shapes and/or matches shapes to words encourage **sight vocabulary recognition** and the ability to make **associations between words** and **objects**. Grouping things according to common attributes such as color, size, shape, etc. (**classification activities**), encourages development of a child's ability to reason and make **logical connections**. **Recognizing number words**, **writing numerals**, and **forming sets of objects** all prepare a child for basic math skills.

CHAPTER 3 Basic Math Skills

Becoming familiar with the **order of numbers from 1-10, learning to write those numbers**, and **understanding the connection between a set of objects and its corresponding numeral** all prepare a child to understand the concepts of addition and subtraction. **Observing and continuing patterns** and **measuring** help children develop logical reasoning skills.

CHAPTER 4 Time and Money

In this chapter children learn about the **numbers on the clock**, and how to **tell time to the hour and half hour**. Children also explore money concepts and use **pennies, nickels** and **dimes**.

CHAPTER 5 Reading Readiness

Determining which items in a group "go together" (**making associations**), and learning to group things according to common attributes (**classification skills**), prepare a child to **notice details**.

CHAPTER 6 Phonics Skills I

This chapter focuses on teaching a child to recognize the initial and final consonant sounds, to learn to write letters and words using these sounds, and to understand the association between sounds, symbols, and words.

CHAPTER 7 Phonics Skills II

Phonics II focuses on training a child to **hear and reproduce the long and short vowel sounds**, as well as the sounds made by combining two letters to make **consonant blends** and **consonant digraphs**.

TABLE OF CONTENTS

HANDWRITING SKILLS

Trace and color the picture.

Skills: Tracing; Fine motor skill development; Eye/hand coordination

TABLE OF CONTENTS

HANDWRITING SKILLS

Trace and color the picture.

Skills: Tracing; Fine motor skill development; Eye/hand coordination

HANDWRITING SKILLS

Trace and color the picture.

Skills: Tracing; Fine motor skill development; Eye/hand coordination

HANDWRITING SKILLS

Trace and color the picture.

Skills: Tracing; Fine motor skill development; Eye/hand coordination

HANDWRITING SKILLS

Trace the broken lines.

Skills: Fine motor skill development; Forming vertical and diagonal lines; Eye/hand coordination

HANDWRITING SKILLS

Trace the broken lines.

Skills: Fine motor skill development; Eye/hand coordination; Corresponding relationships

HANDWRITING SKILLS

Start at the dots. Trace the broken lines. Then finish the page.

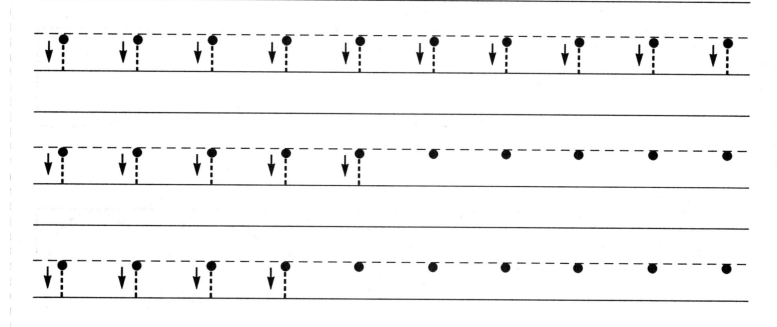

Skills: Fine motor skill development; Eye/hand coordination; Forming vertical lines

HANDWRITING SKILLS

Start at the dots. Trace the broken lines. Then finish the page.

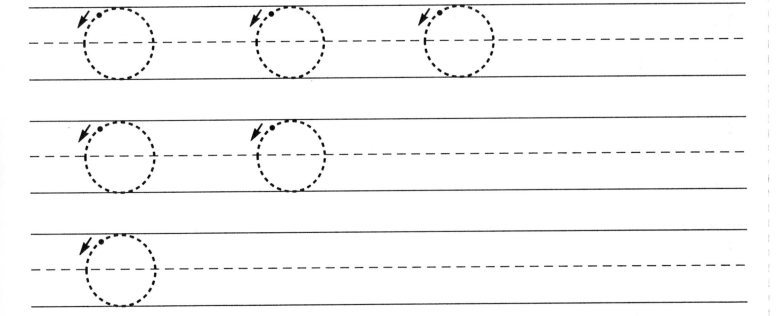

Skills: Fine motor skill development; Eye/hand coordination; Forming closed curves

HANDWRITING SKILLS

Start at the dots. Trace the broken lines. Then finish the page.

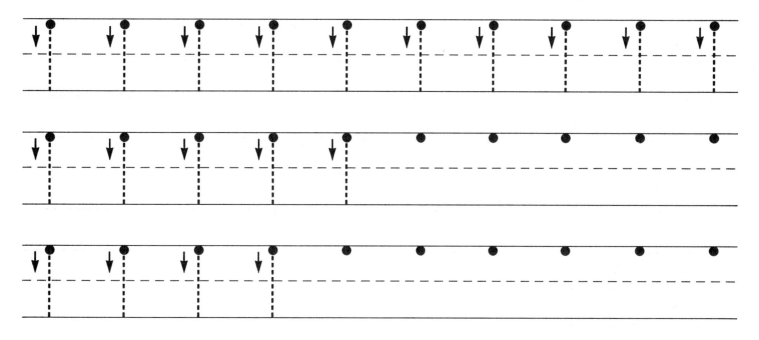

Skills: Fine motor skill development; Eye/hand coordination; Forming vertical lines

HANDWRITING SKILLS

Start at the dots. Trace the broken lines. Then finish the page.

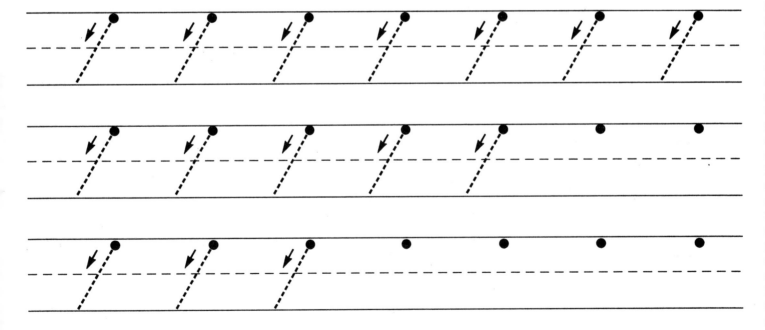

Skills: Fine motor skill development; Eye/hand coordination; Forming diagonal lines

HANDWRITING SKILLS

Start at the dots. Trace the broken lines. Then finish the page.

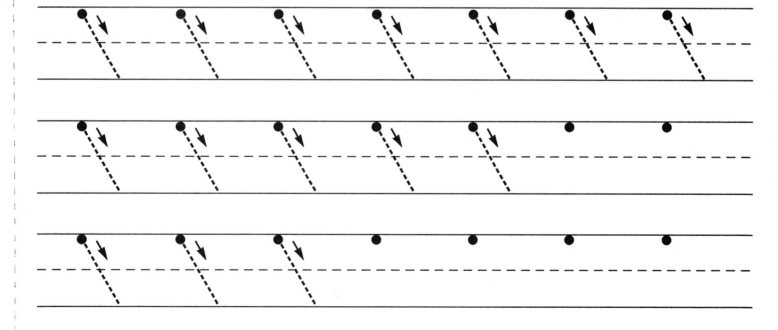

Skills: Fine motor skill development; Eye/hand coordination; Forming diagonal lines

HANDWRITING SKILLS

Start at the dots. Trace the broken lines. Then finish the page.

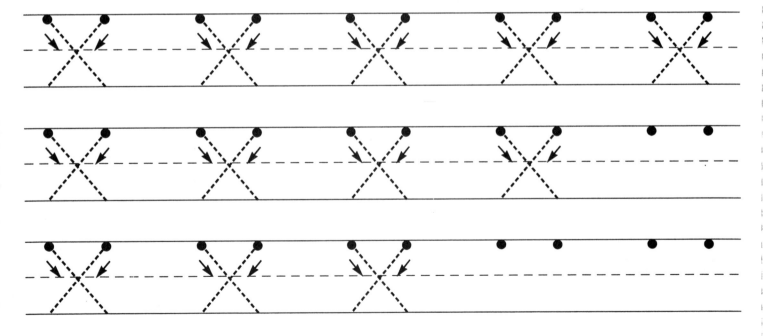

Skills: Fine motor skill development; Eye/hand coordination

HANDWRITING SKILLS

Start at the dots. Trace the broken lines. Then finish the page.

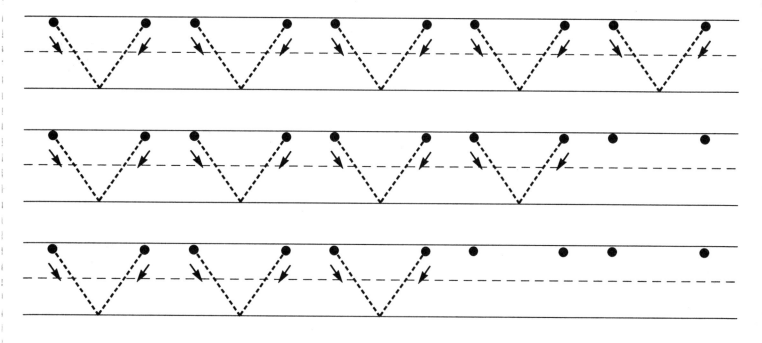

Skills: Fine motor skill development; Eye/hand coordination

HANDWRITING SKILLS

Start at the dots. Trace the broken lines. Then finish the page.

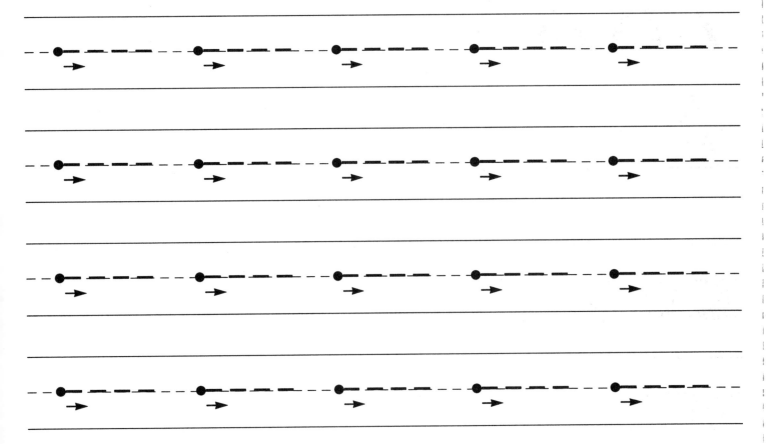

Skills: Fine motor skill development; Eye/hand coordination; Forming horizontal lines

HANDWRITING SKILLS

Follow the directions of each arrow. Then practice writing each letter.

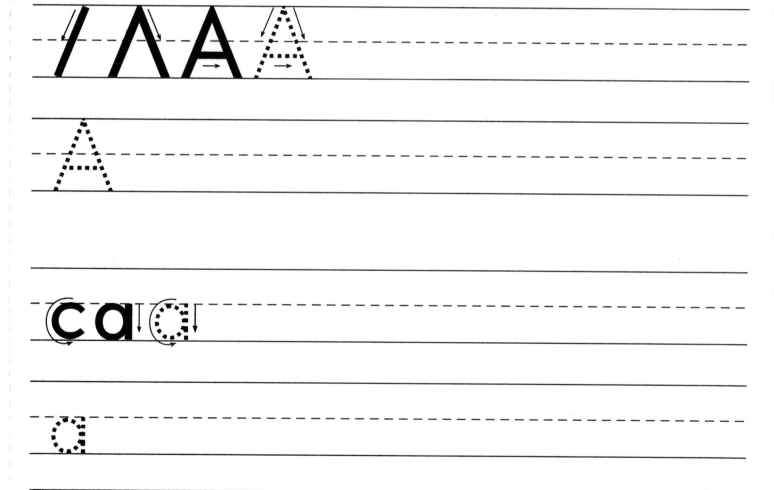

Skills: Forming upper/lower case "a"; Writing left to right

HANDWRITING SKILLS

Follow the directions of each arrow. Then practice writing each letter.

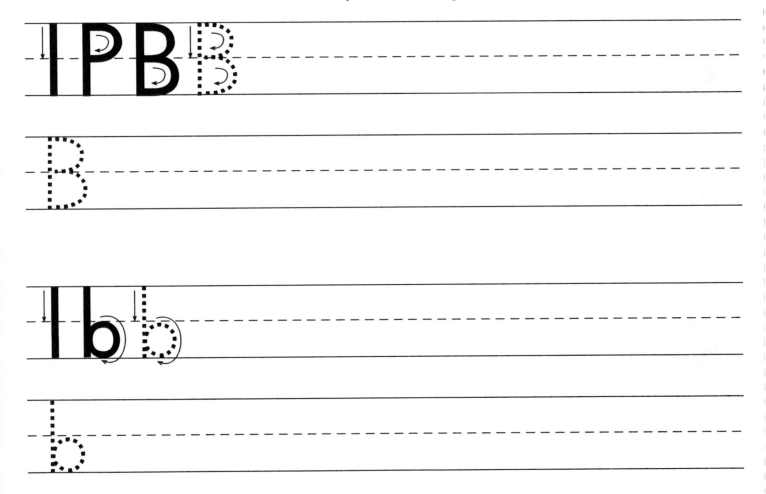

Skills: Forming upper/lower case "b"; Writing left to right

HANDWRITING SKILLS

Follow the directions of each arrow. Then practice writing each letter.

Skills: Forming upper/lower case "c"; Writing left to right

HANDWRITING SKILLS

Follow the directions of each arrow. Then practice writing each letter.

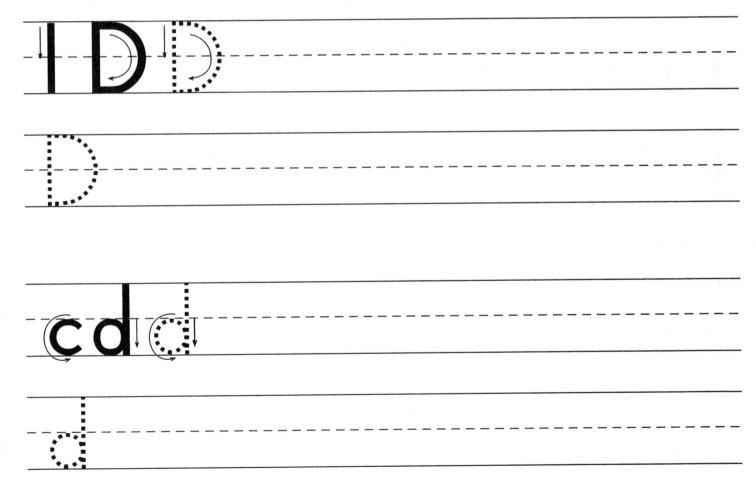

Skills: Forming upper/lower case "d"; Writing left to right

HANDWRITING SKILLS

Follow the directions of each arrow. Then practice writing each letter.

Skills: Forming upper/lower case "e"; Writing left to right

HANDWRITING SKILLS

Follow the directions of each arrow. Then practice writing each letter.

Skills: Forming upper/lower case "f"; Writing left to right

HANDWRITING SKILLS

Follow the directions of each arrow. Then practice writing each letter.

Skills: Forming upper/lower case "g"; Writing left to right

HANDWRITING SKILLS

Follow the directions of each arrow. Then practice writing each letter.

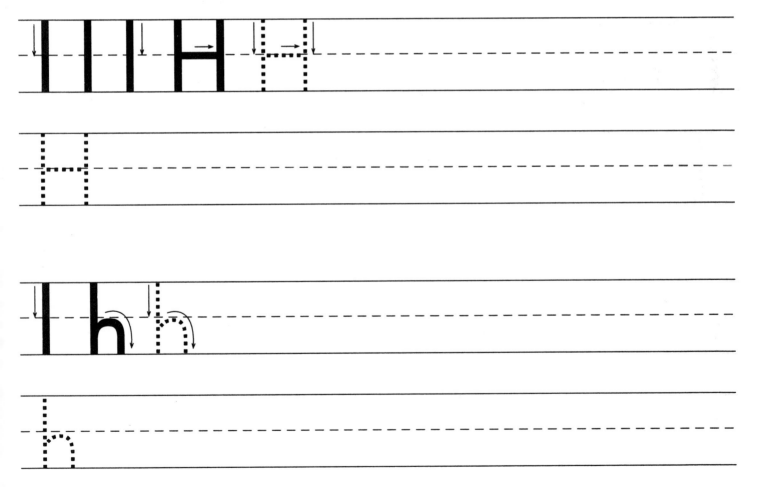

Skills: Forming upper/lower case "h"; Writing left to right

HANDWRITING SKILLS

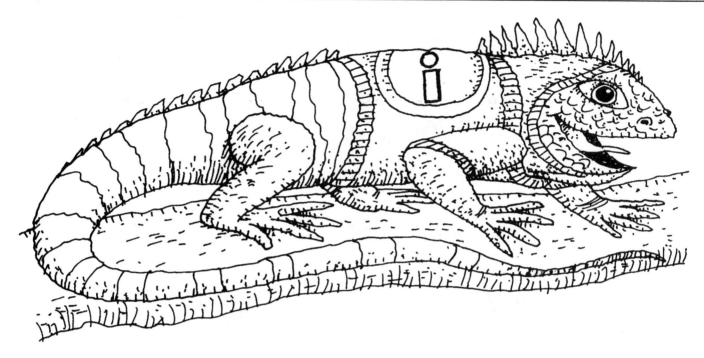

Follow the directions of each arrow. Then practice writing each letter.

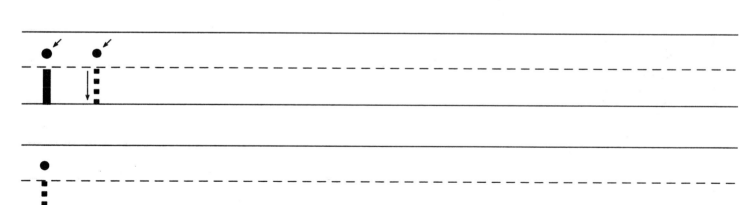

Skills: Forming upper/lower case "i"; Writing left to right

HANDWRITING SKILLS

Follow the directions of each arrow. Then practice writing each letter.

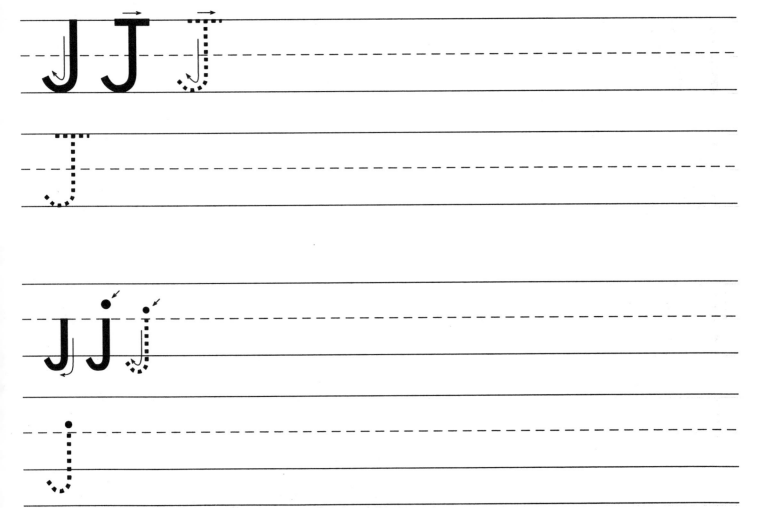

Skills: Forming upper/lower case "j"; Writing left to right

Follow the directions of each arrow. Then practice writing each letter.

Skills: Forming upper/lower case "k"; Writing left to right

HANDWRITING SKILLS

Follow the directions of each arrow. Then practice writing each letter.

Skills: Forming upper/lower case "l"; Writing left to right

HANDWRITING SKILLS

Follow the directions of each arrow. Then practice writing each letter.

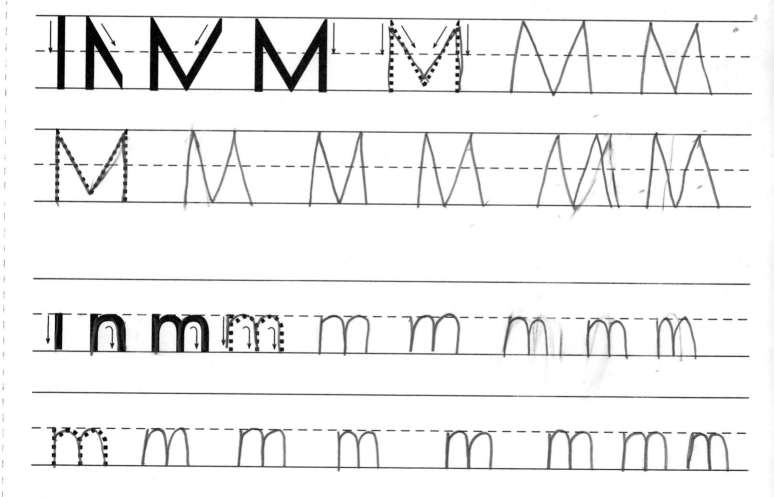

Skills: Forming upper/lower case "m"; Writing left to right

HANDWRITING SKILLS

Follow the directions of each arrow. Then practice writing each letter.

Skills: Forming upper/lower case "n"; Writing left to right

HANDWRITING SKILLS

Follow the directions of each arrow. Then practice writing each letter.

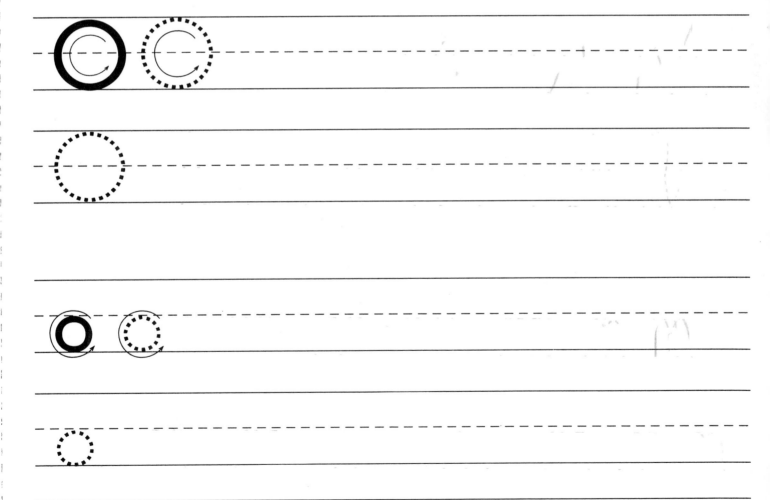

Skills: Forming upper/lower case "o"; Writing left to right

HANDWRITING SKILLS

Follow the directions of each arrow. Then practice writing each letter.

Skills: Forming upper/lower case "p"; Writing left to right

HANDWRITING SKILLS

Follow the directions of each arrow. Then practice writing each letter.

Skills: Forming upper/lower case "q"; Writing left to right

Follow the directions of each arrow. Then practice writing each letter.

Skills: Forming upper/lower case "r"; Writing left to right

HANDWRITING SKILLS

Follow the directions of each arrow. Then practice writing each letter.

Skills: Forming upper/lower case "s"; Writing left to right

HANDWRITING SKILLS

Follow the directions of each arrow. Then practice writing each letter.

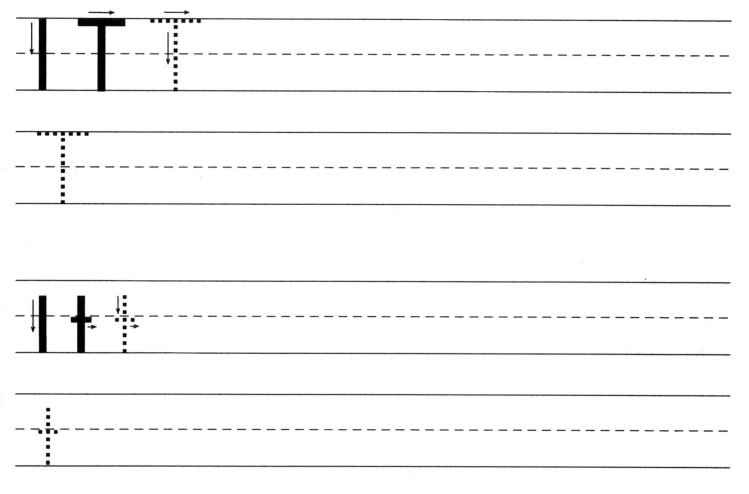

Skills: Forming upper/lower case "t"; Writing left to right

HANDWRITING SKILLS

Follow the directions of each arrow. Then practice writing each letter.

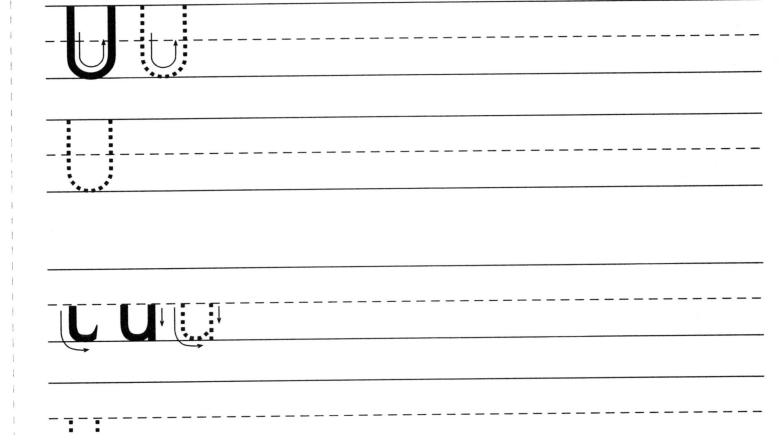

Skills: Forming upper/lower case "u"; Writing left to right

HANDWRITING SKILLS

Follow the directions of each arrow. Then practice writing each letter.

Skills: Forming upper/lower case "v"; Writing left to right

HANDWRITING SKILLS

Follow the directions of each arrow. Then practice writing each letter.

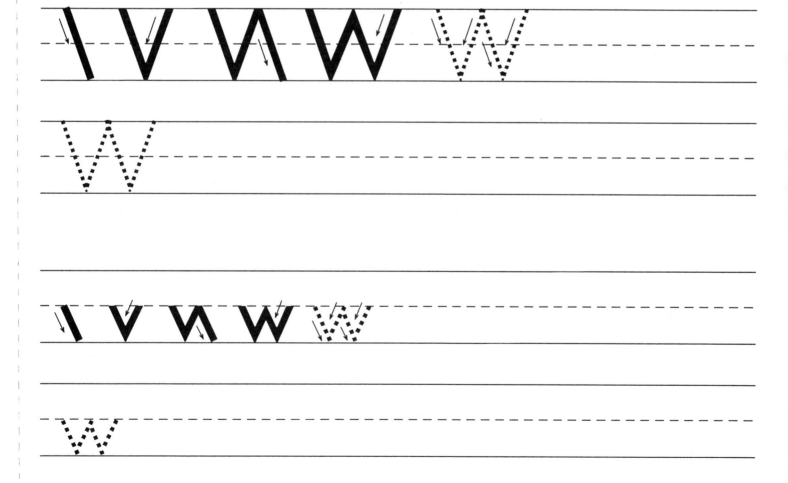

Skills: Forming upper/lower case "w"; Writing left to right

HANDWRITING SKILLS

Follow the directions of each arrow. Then practice writing each letter.

Skills: Forming upper/lower case "x"; Writing left to right

HANDWRITING SKILLS

Follow the directions of each arrow. Then practice writing each letter.

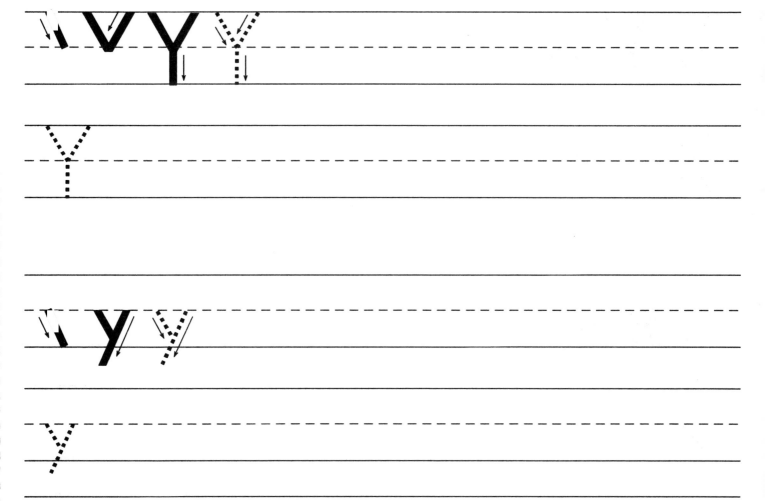

Skills: Forming upper/lower case "y"; Writing left to right

HANDWRITING SKILLS

Follow the directions of each arrow. Then practice writing each letter.

Skills: Forming upper/lower case "z"; Writing left to right

yellow

yellow

Color these things that are yellow.

y

Skills: Distinguishing color; Classification; Word recognition

blue

Color these things that are blue.

blue

b

Skills: Distinguishing color; Classification; Word recognition

orange

orange

Color these things that are orange.

o

Skills: Distinguishing color; Classification; Word recognition

purple

purple

Color these things that are purple.

p

Skills: Distinguishing color; Classification; Word recognition

green

green

Color these things that are green.

g

black

black

Color these things that are black.

b

brown

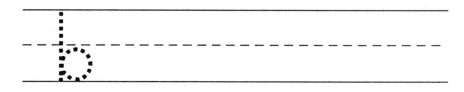

Color these things that are brown.

Skills: Distinguishing color; Classification; Word recognition

gray

Color these things that are gray.

gray

g

Skills: Distinguishing color; Classification; Word recognition

COLORS, SHAPES, AND NUMBERS

Color the rainbow.

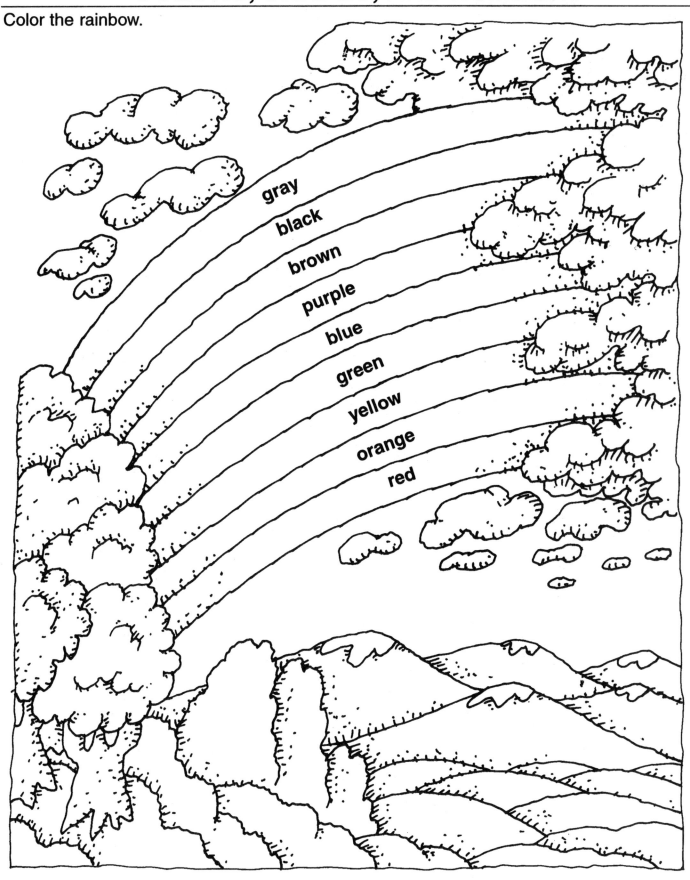

gray

black

brown

purple

blue

green

yellow

orange

red

Skills: Visual memory of sight vocabulary; Following directions

Look at the square.
Then trace, print, and draw.

square

Draw 1 square. Color it blue.

Skills: Fine motor skill development; Sight vocabulary recognition; Association between sight vocabulary and shapes

COLORS, SHAPES, AND NUMBERS

Look at the circle.
Then trace, print, and draw.

circle

circle

Draw 1 circle. Color it brown.

Skills: Fine motor skill development; Sight vocabulary recognition; Association between sight vocabulary and shapes

Look at the rectangle.
Then trace, print, and draw.

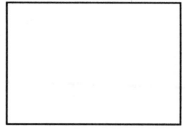

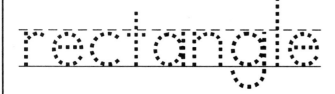

Draw 1 rectangle. Color it yellow.

Skills: Fine motor skill development; Sight vocabulary recognition; Association between sight vocabulary and shapes

COLORS, SHAPES, AND NUMBERS

Look at the triangle.
Then trace, print, and draw.

triangle

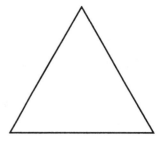

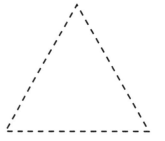

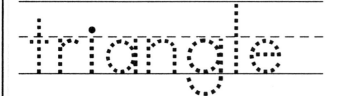

Draw 1 triangle. Color it green.

Skills: Fine motor skill development; Sight vocabulary recognition; Association between sight vocabulary and shapes

COLORS, SHAPES, AND NUMBERS

Match the shape to the word.   Match the word to the shape.

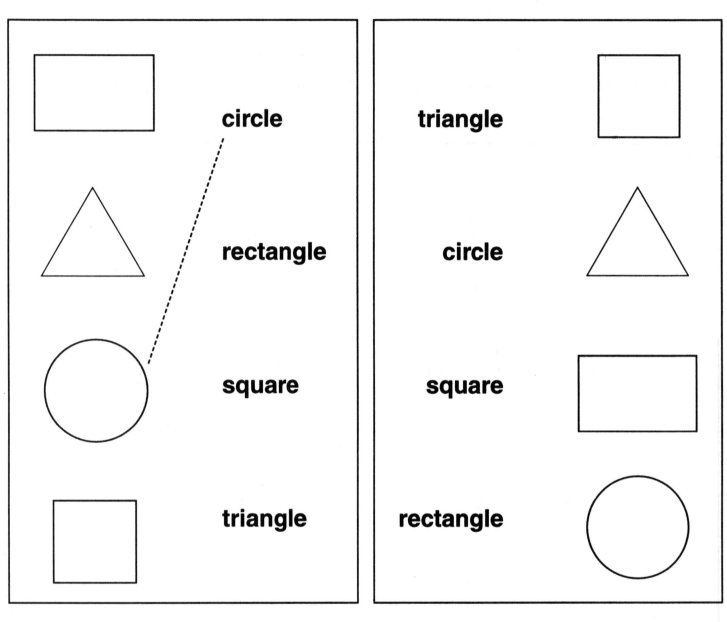

Color the △ triangles red.
Color the ○ circles yellow.
Color the ▭ rectangles green.
Color the □ squares blue.

Skills: Following directions; Association between sight vocabulary and shapes; Sight vocabulary recognition

COLORS, SHAPES, AND NUMBERS

Print the word. Color the shape.

square   rectangle   triangle   circle

_____

- - - - - - - - - - - - - -

_____

_____

- - - - - - - - - - - - - -

_____

_____

- - - - - - - - - - - - - -

_____

_____

- - - - - - - - - - - - - -

_____

Skills: Association between sight vocabulary and shapes; Practice writing skills; Sight vocabulary recognition

COLORS, SHAPES, AND NUMBERS

Circle the correct numeral.

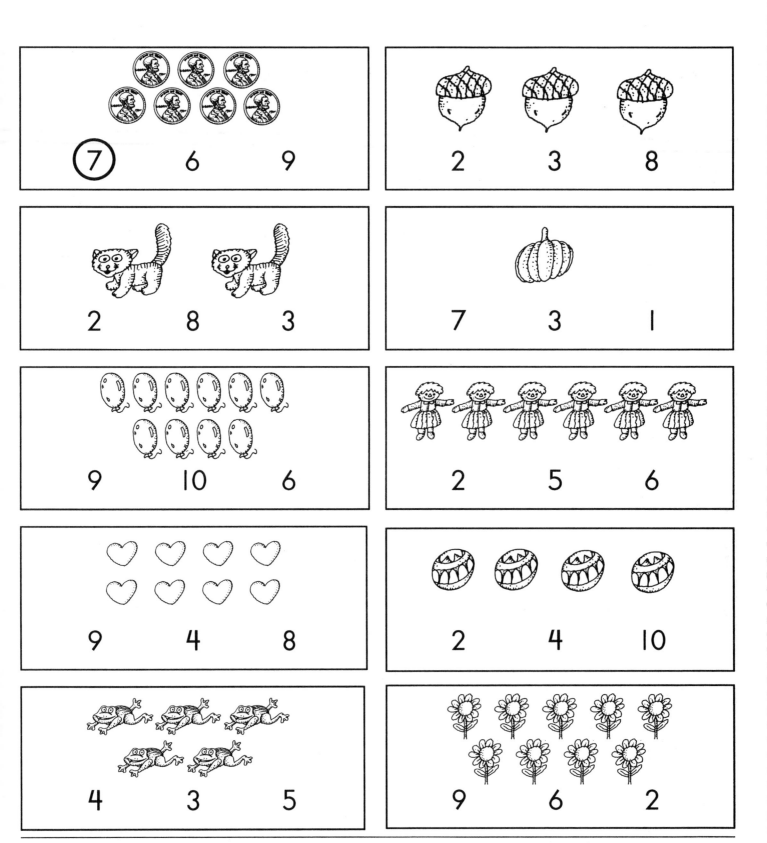

Skills: Recognizing sets of objects and the corresponding numeral; Following directions

COLORS, SHAPES, AND NUMBERS

Print the correct numeral.

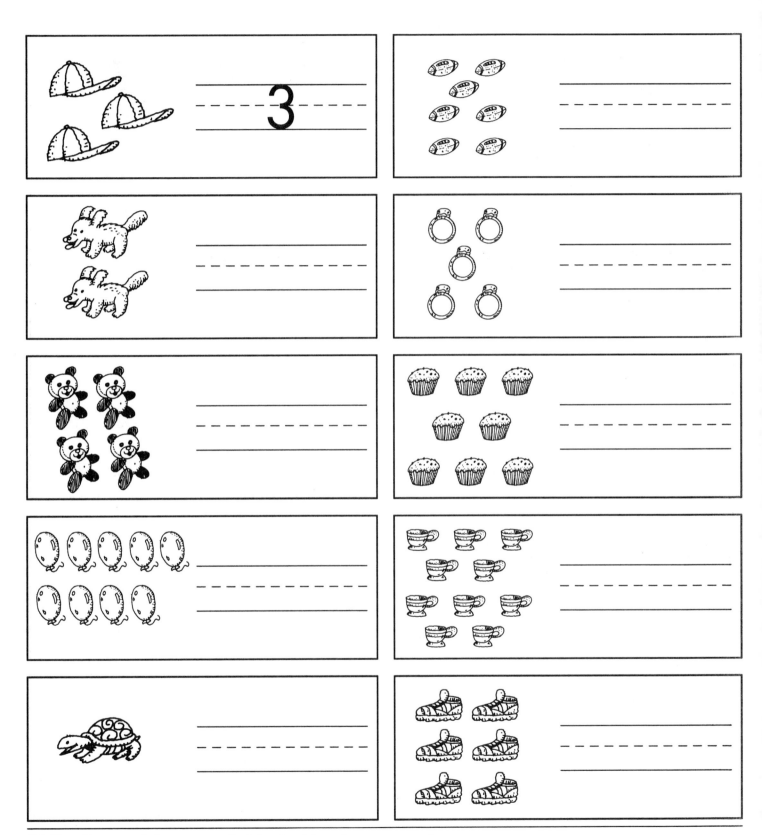

Skills: Recognizing sets of objects; Forming numerals

COLORS, SHAPES, AND NUMBERS

Trace and print the words and numerals.

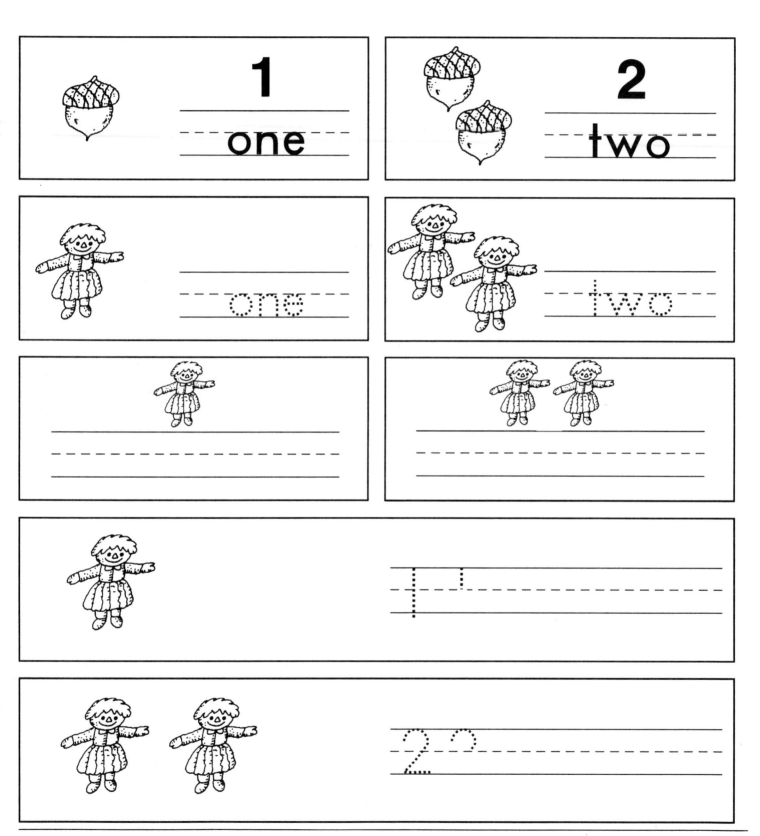

Skills: Recognizing sets of 1 and 2; Association between sight vocabulary, numerals, and sets

COLORS, SHAPES, AND NUMBERS

Trace and print the words and numerals.

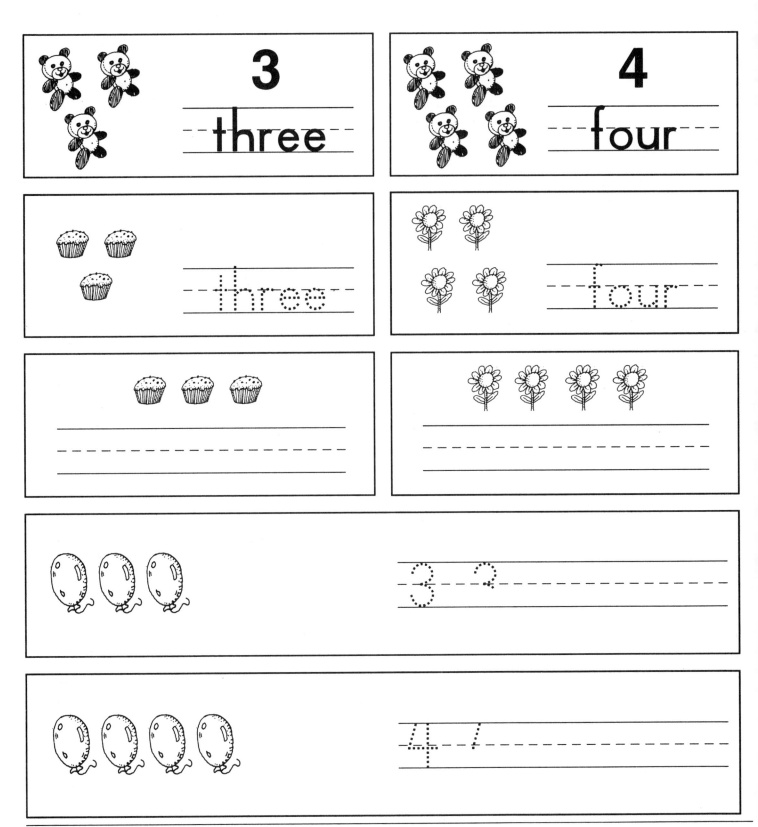

Skills: Recognizing sets of 3 and 4; Association between sight vocabulary, numerals, and sets

COLORS, SHAPES, AND NUMBERS

Trace and print the words and numerals.

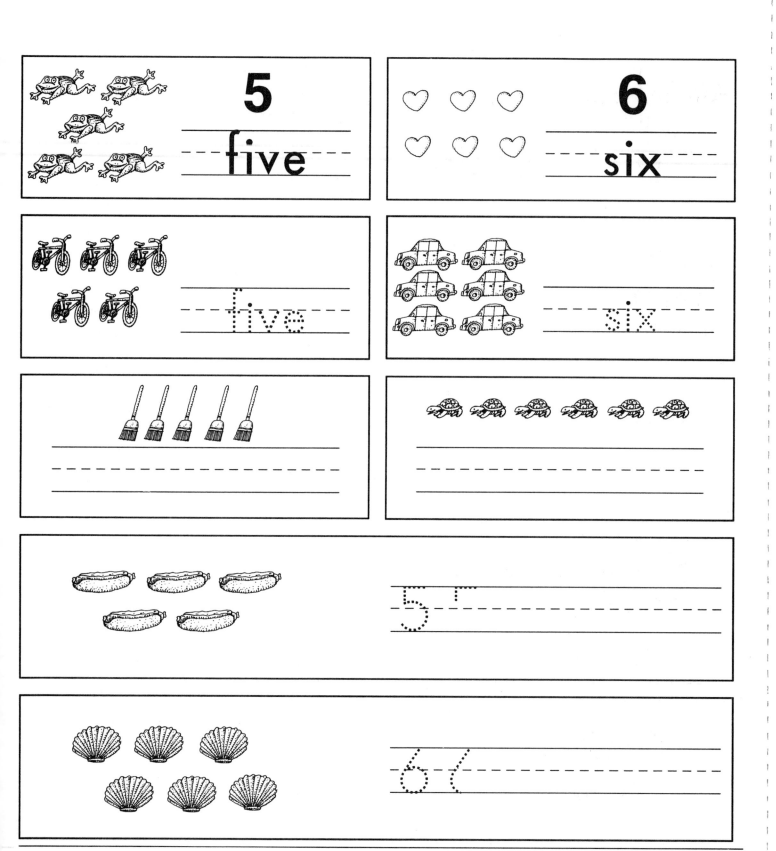

Skills: Recognizing sets of 5 and 6; Association between sight vocabulary, numerals, and sets

COLORS, SHAPES, AND NUMBERS

Trace and print the words and numerals.

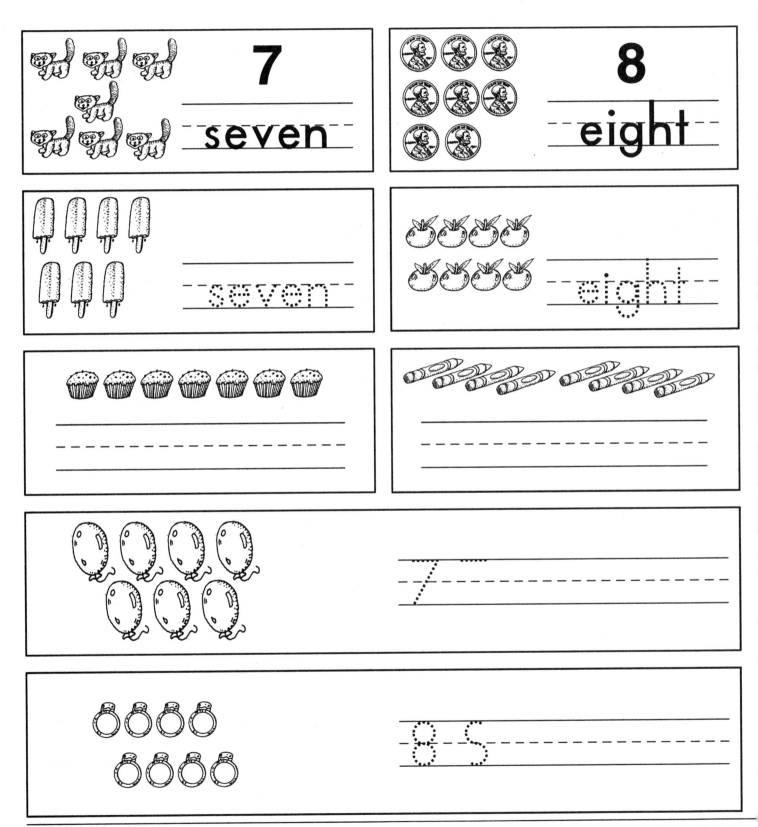

Skills: Recognizing sets of 7 and 8; Association between sight vocabulary, numerals, and sets

COLORS, SHAPES, AND NUMBERS

Trace and print the words and numerals.

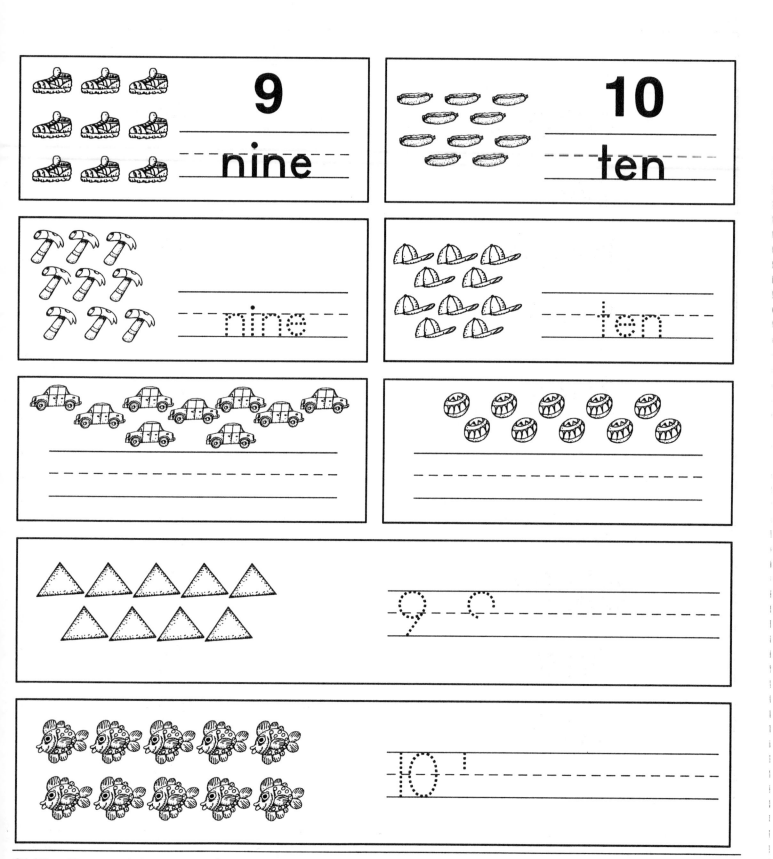

Skills: Recognizing sets of 9 and 10; Association between sight vocabulary, numerals, and sets

COLORS, SHAPES, AND NUMBERS

Match the words and numerals.

one	6
two	1
three	8
four	2
five	4
six	3
seven	9
eight	7
nine	5
ten	10

Skills: Recognizing numerals and the corresponding number word

COLORS, SHAPES, AND NUMBERS

Circle the correct word.

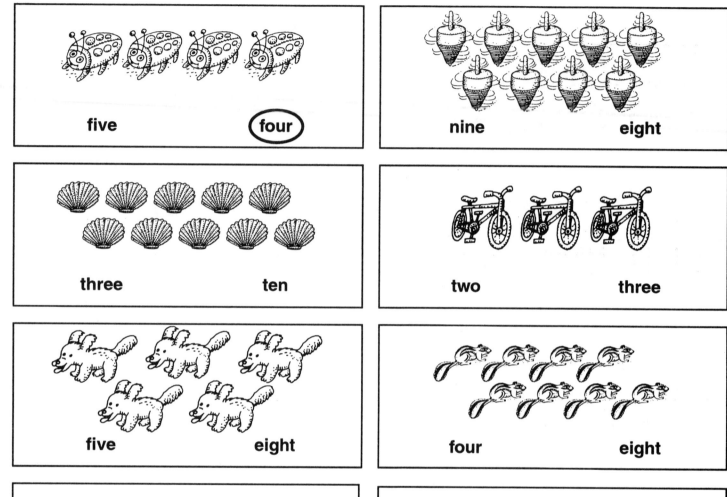

five   (four)

nine   eight

three   ten

two   three

five   eight

four   eight

two   five

six   nine

six   seven

seven   one

Skills: Recognizing sets of objects and the corresponding number word

COLORS, SHAPES, AND NUMBERS

Trace the word. Print the numeral. Draw the correct number of diamonds.

Skills: Recognizing number words and writing numerals. Forming corresponding sets of objects

COLORS, SHAPES, AND NUMBERS

Trace the word. Print the numeral. Draw the correct number of squares.

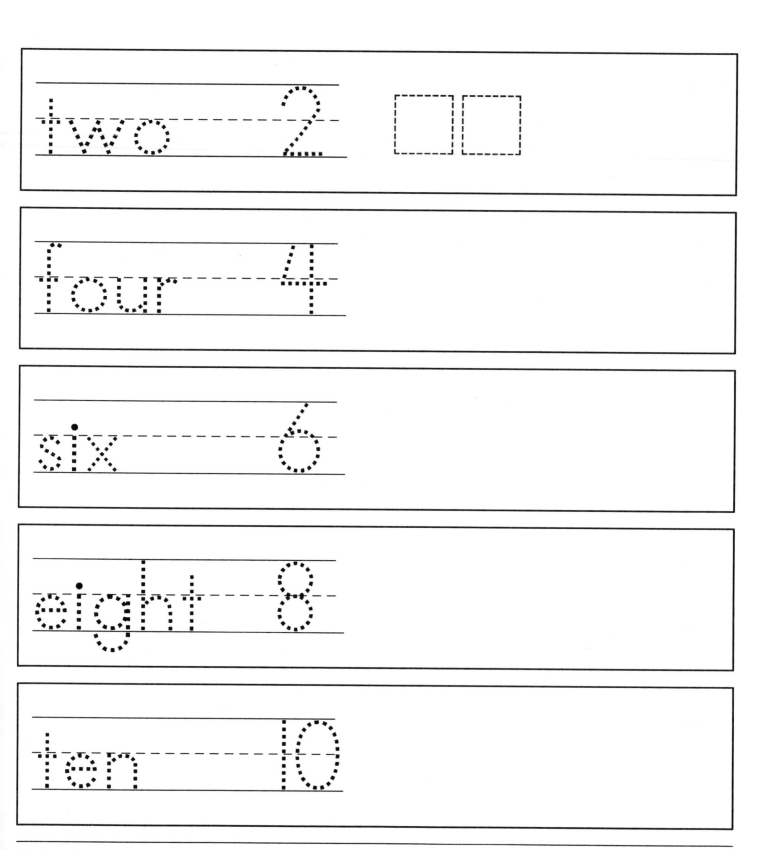

Skills: Recognizing number words and writing numerals; Forming corresponding sets of objects

COLORS, SHAPES, AND NUMBERS

Trace the numeral. Print the word. Draw the correct number of boxes.

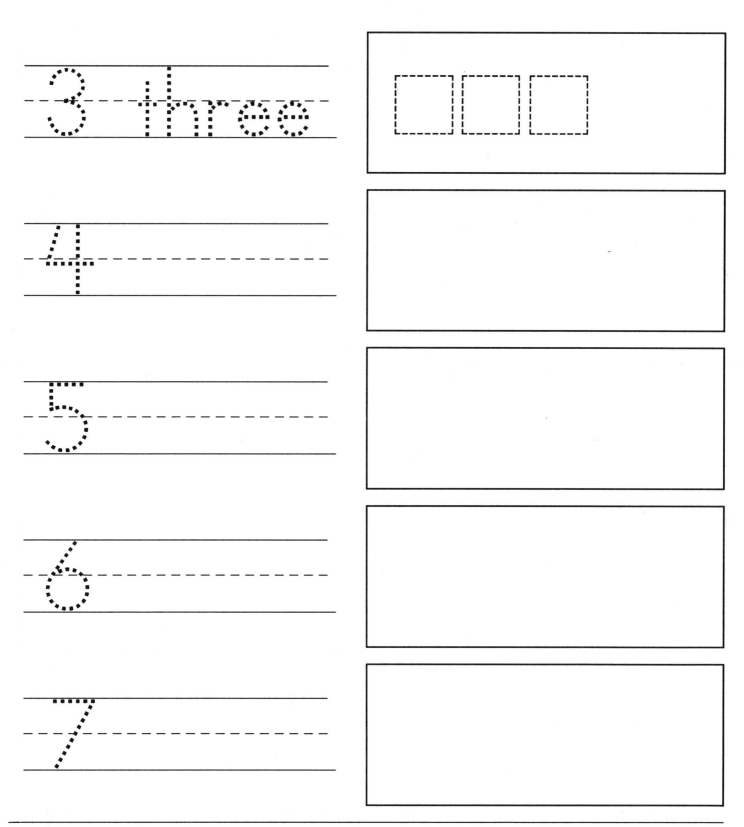

Skills: Recognizing numerals; Writing number words; Forming corresponding sets of objects

COLORS, SHAPES, AND NUMBERS

Trace the numeral. Print the word. Draw the correct number of boxes.

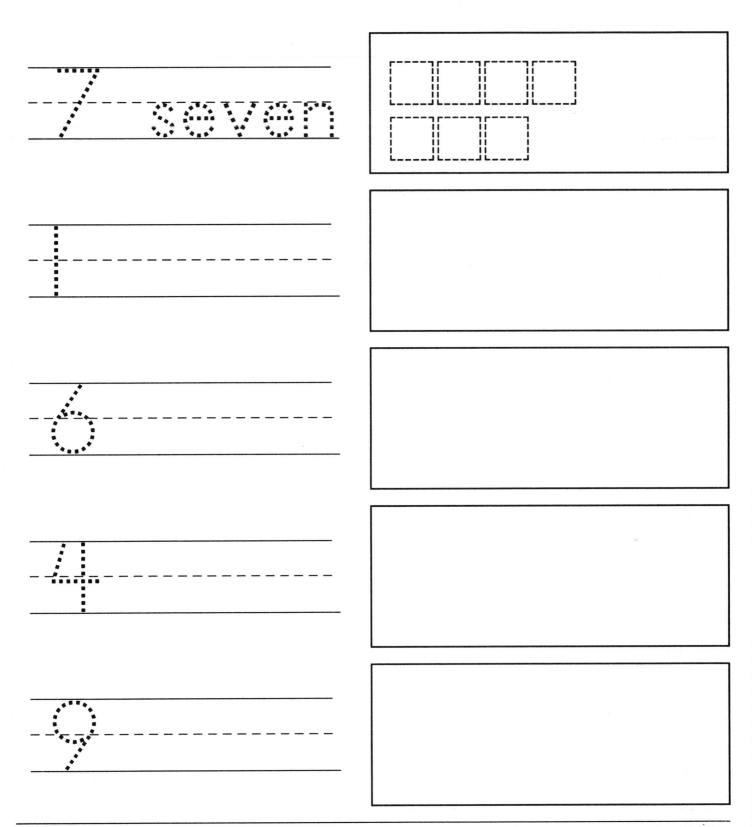

COLORS, SHAPES, AND NUMBERS

Trace the numeral. Match the numeral with the correct number of shapes. Print the word.

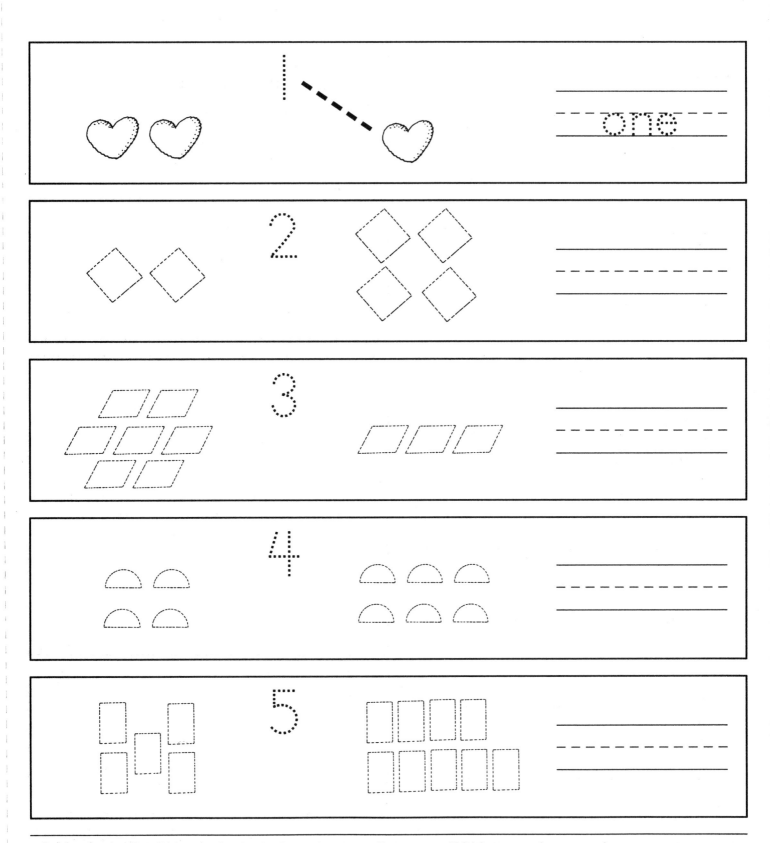

Skills: Matching numerals to their corresponding sets; Writing number words

COLORS, SHAPES, AND NUMBERS

Trace the numeral. Match the numeral with the correct number of objects. Print the word.

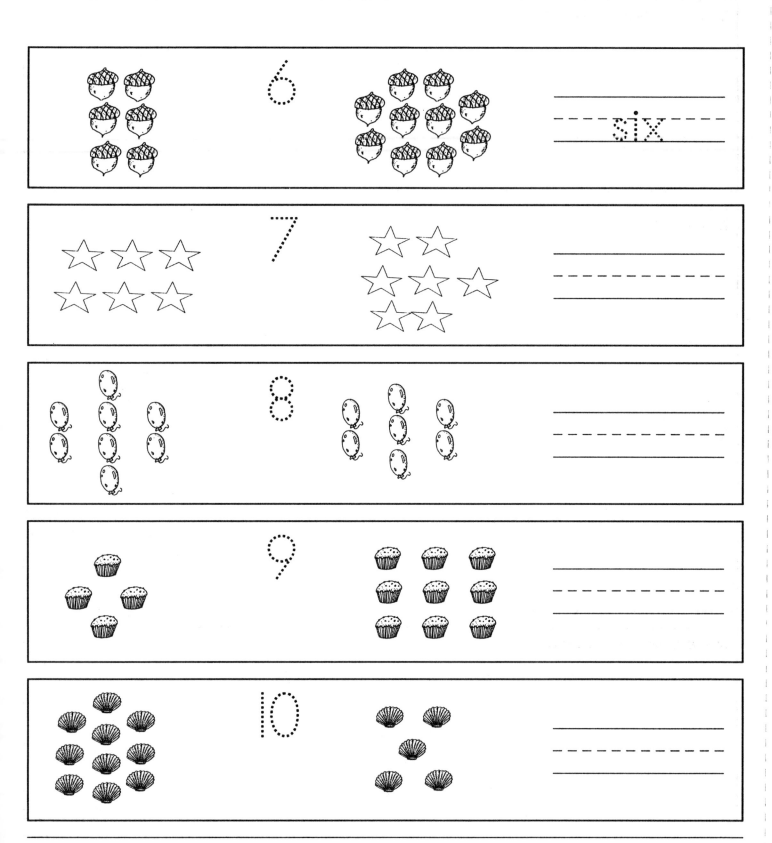

six

COLORS, SHAPES, AND NUMBERS

Make 1 green ☐ square.

Make 2 red ○ circles.

Make 3 blue ☐ rectangles.

Make 4 yellow △ triangles.

Skills: Following directions; Understanding number, shape, and color; Fine motor
skill development

COLORS, SHAPES, AND NUMBERS

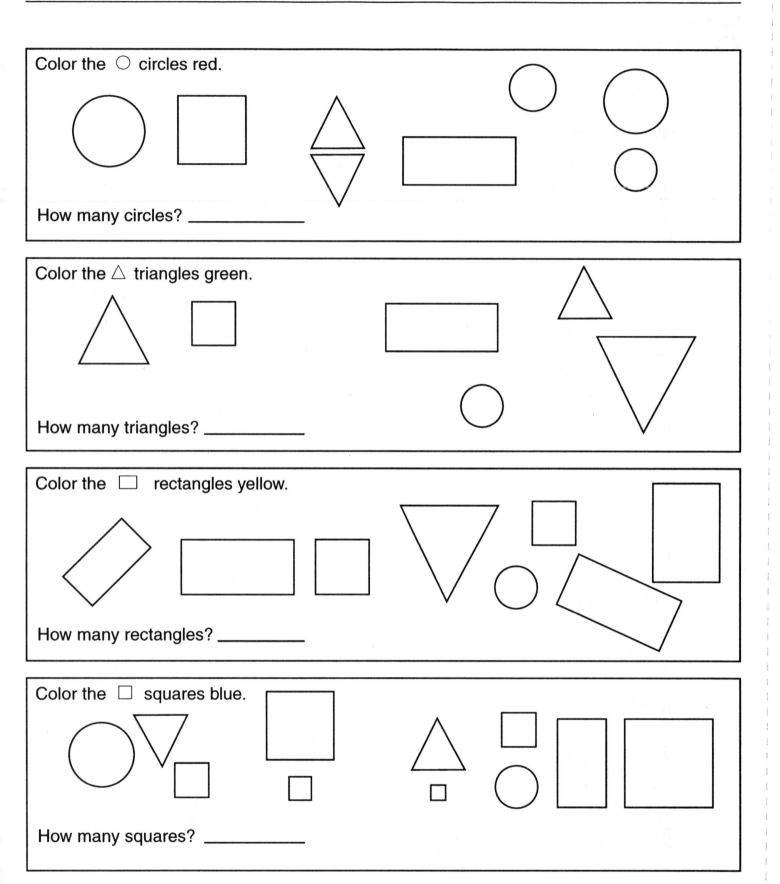

Color the ○ circles red.

How many circles? _____

Color the △ triangles green.

How many triangles? _____

Color the □ rectangles yellow.

How many rectangles? _____

Color the □ squares blue.

How many squares? _____

Skills: Following directions; Understanding color, shape, and number; Noticing attributes

BASIC MATH SKILLS

Look at each butterfly.
What number comes next?

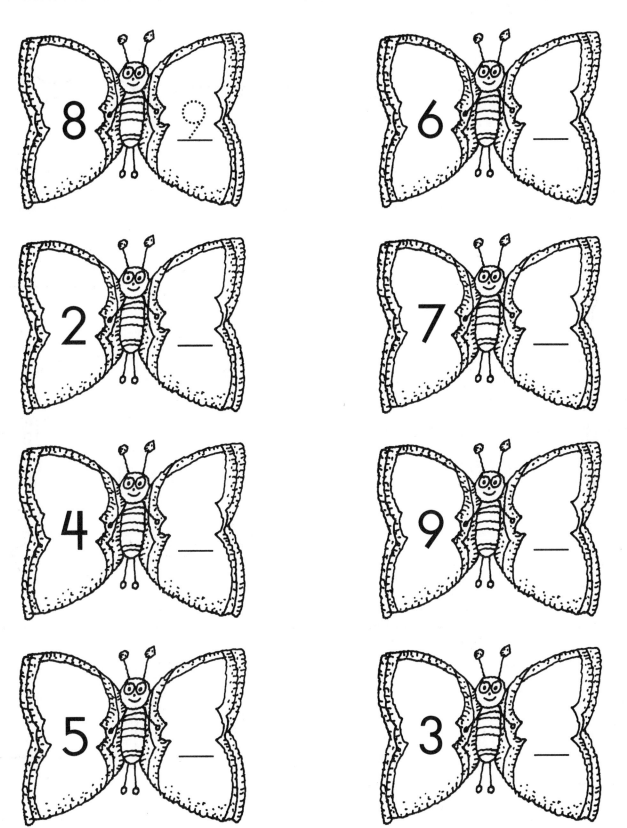

Skills: Ordering numbers to 10; Writing numerals

BASIC MATH SKILLS

Look at each group of cupcakes.
What number comes between?

BASIC MATH SKILLS

Look at the stars.
Write the missing numbers.

BASIC MATH SKILLS

Look at each picture.
How many are in the first group?

How many are in the second group?
How many in all?

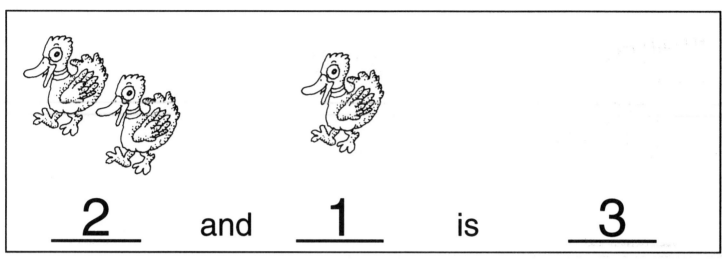

__2__ and __1__ is __3__

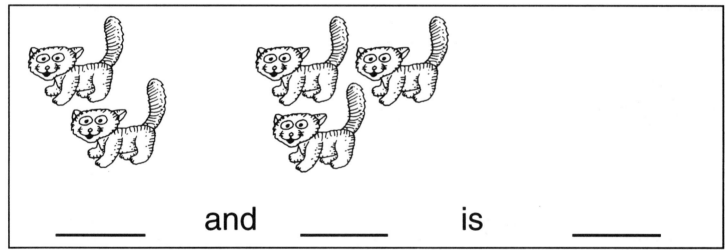

_____ and _____ is _____

_____ and _____ is _____

Skills: Recognizing sets of objects and writing corresponding numerals; Adding groups of objects

BASIC MATH SKILLS

Look at each picture.
How many are in the first group?

How many are in the second group?
How many in all?

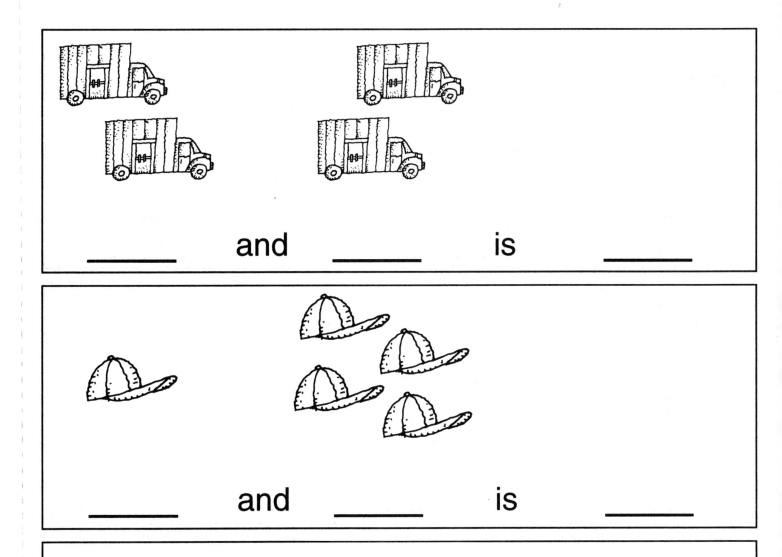

_____ and _____ is _____

_____ and _____ is _____

_____ and _____ is _____

Skills: Recognizing sets of objects and writing corresponding numerals; Adding groups of objects

BASIC MATH SKILLS

Look at each picture.
How many are in the first group?

How many are in the second group?
How many in all?

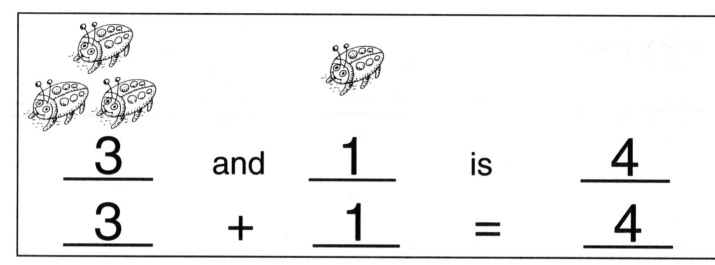

$$3 \text{ and } 1 \text{ is } 4$$

$$3 + 1 = 4$$

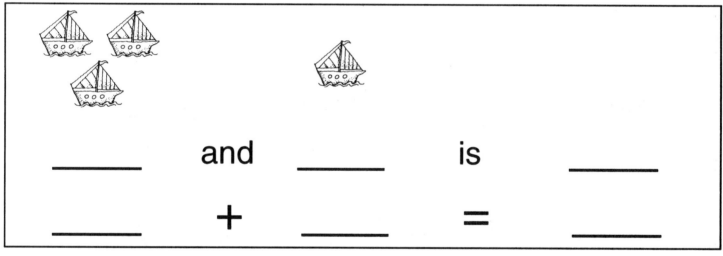

_____ and _____ is _____

_____ + _____ = _____

_____ and _____ is _____

_____ + _____ = _____

Skills: Recognizing sets of objects and writing corresponding numerals; Adding groups of objects; Understanding addition sentences

BASIC MATH SKILLS

Look at each picture.
How many are in the first group?

How many are in the second group?
How many in all?

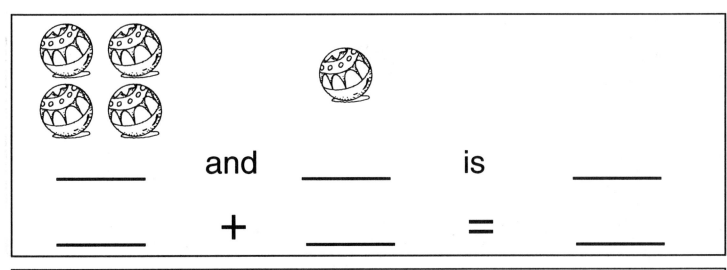

_____ and _____ is _____

_____ + _____ = _____

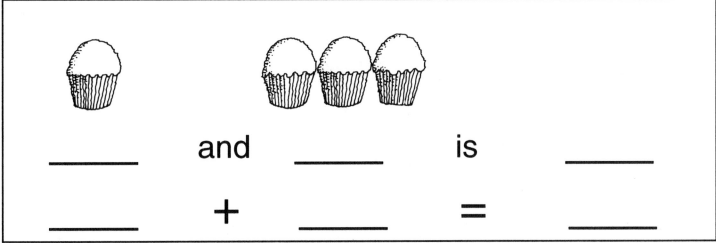

_____ and _____ is _____

_____ + _____ = _____

_____ and _____ is _____

_____ + _____ = _____

Skills: Recognizing sets of objects and writing corresponding numerals; Adding groups of objects; Understanding addition sentences

BASIC MATH SKILLS

Look at each picture.
How many are in the first group?

How many are in the second group?
How many in all?

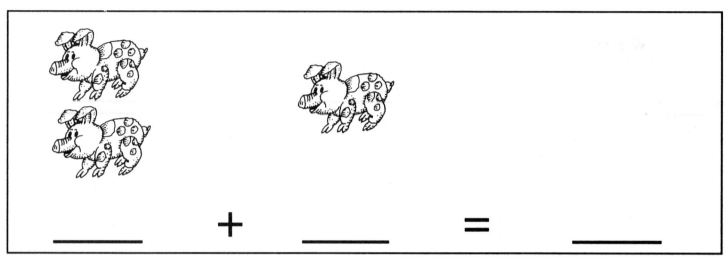

_____   **+**   _____   **=**   _____

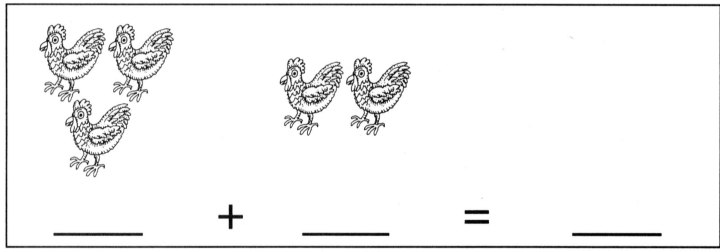

_____   **+**   _____   **=**   _____

_____   **+**   _____   **=**   _____

Skills: Recognizing sets of objects and writing corresponding numerals; Adding groups of objects; Practicing addition problems

BASIC MATH SKILLS

Look at each picture.
How many are in the first group?

How many are in the second group?
How many in all?

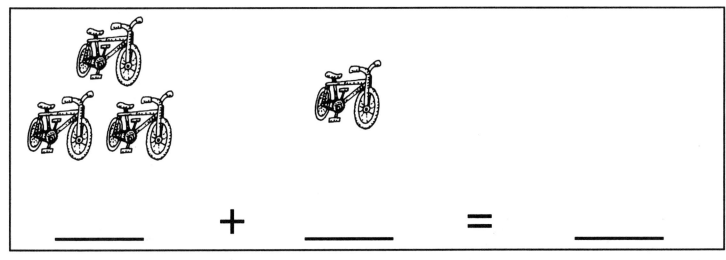

_____ + _____ = _____

_____ + _____ = _____

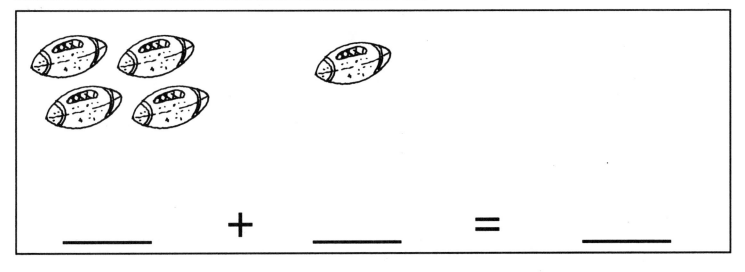

_____ + _____ = _____

Skills: Recognizing sets of objects and writing corresponding numerals; Adding groups of objects; Practicing addition problems

BASIC MATH SKILLS

Look at each picture.
How many are in the first group?

How many are in the second group?
How many in all?

$$3 \quad + \quad 2 \quad = \quad \underline{}$$

$$4 \quad + \quad 1 \quad = \quad \underline{}$$

$$1 \quad + \quad 2 \quad = \quad \underline{}$$

Skills: Recognizing sets of objects and writing corresponding numerals; Adding groups of objects; Practicing addition problems

BASIC MATH SKILLS

How many in all?
Add to find out.

$$\begin{array}{r} 2 \\ +1 \\ \hline \end{array}$$

$$\begin{array}{r} 3 \\ +2 \\ \hline \end{array}$$

$$\begin{array}{r} 1 \\ +4 \\ \hline \end{array}$$

$$\begin{array}{r} 3 \\ +1 \\ \hline \end{array}$$

Skills: Solving vertical addition problems; Writing numerals

BASIC MATH SKILLS

How many in all?
Add to find out.

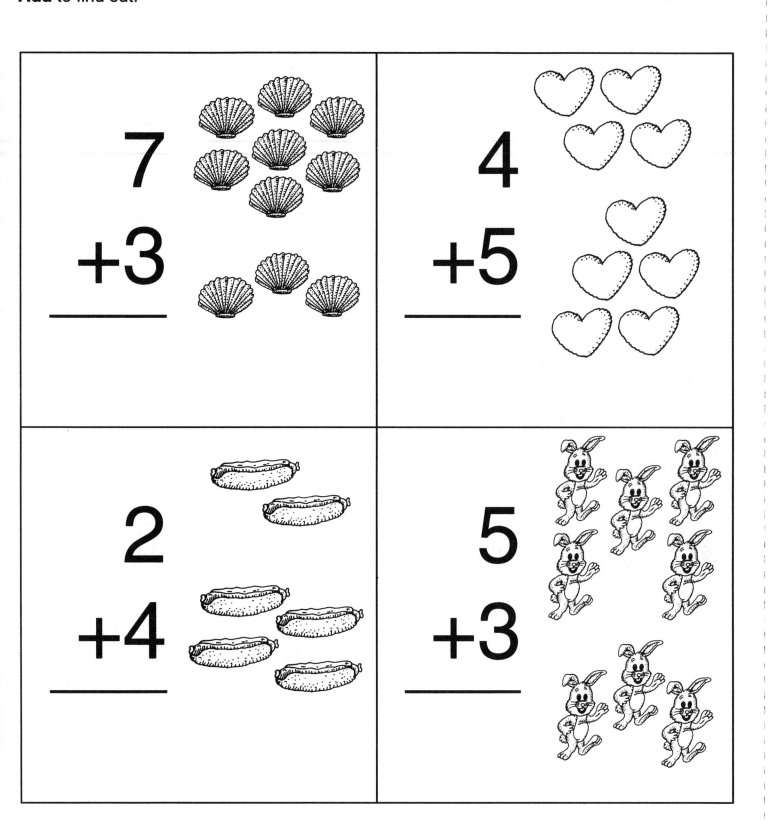

$$\begin{array}{r}7\\+3\\\hline\end{array}$$

$$\begin{array}{r}4\\+5\\\hline\end{array}$$

$$\begin{array}{r}2\\+4\\\hline\end{array}$$

$$\begin{array}{r}5\\+3\\\hline\end{array}$$

Skills: Solving vertical addition problems; Writing numerals

BASIC MATH SKILLS

How many in all?
Add to find out.

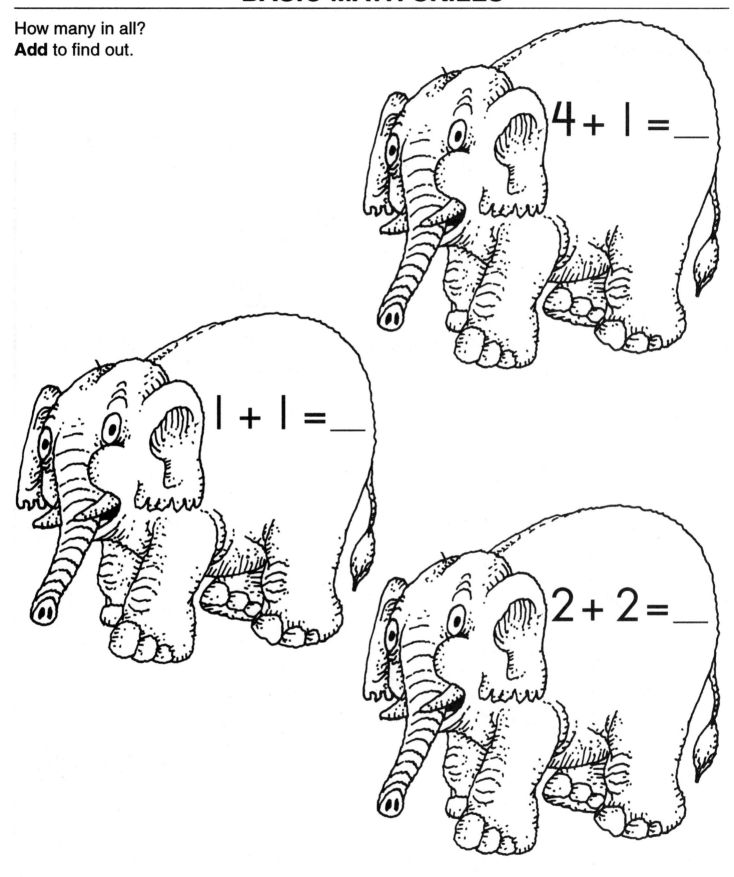

$4 + 1 = \underline{}$

$1 + 1 = \underline{}$

$2 + 2 = \underline{}$

Skills: Solving addition sentences; Writing numerals

BASIC MATH SKILLS

Add the numbers in each sun.
If the answer is 5, color it red.
If the answer is 4, color it blue.
If the answer is 3, color it yellow.

Skills: Solving vertical addition problems; Writing numerals

BASIC MATH SKILLS

Add. Then color each picture.

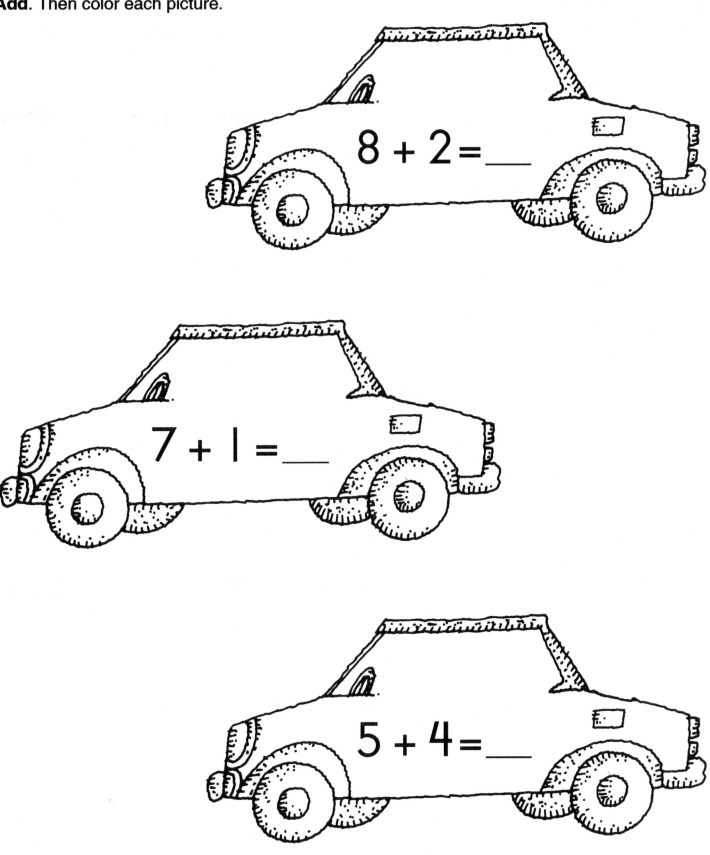

$8 + 2 = \underline{}$

$7 + 1 = \underline{}$

$5 + 4 = \underline{}$

Skills: Solving addition problems; Writing numerals

BASIC MATH SKILLS

Look at each picture.
How many are left?

__3__ take away __1__ is __2__

__5__ take away __2__ is __3__

__4__ take away __3__ is __1__

Skills: Recognizing sets of objects and writing corresponding numerals; Subtracting groups of objects

BASIC MATH SKILLS

Look at each picture.
How many are left?

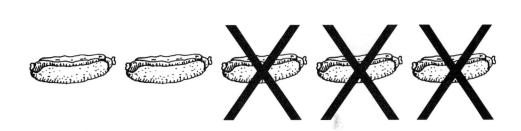

__5__   take away   __3__   is   __2__

__4__   take away   __1__   is   __3__

__2__   take away   __1__   is   __1__

Skills: Recognizing sets of objects and writing corresponding numerals; Subtracting groups of objects

BASIC MATH SKILLS

Look at each picture.
How many are left?

$$\underline{\quad 5 \quad} \text{ take away } \underline{\quad \text{12} \quad} \text{ is } \underline{\quad 3 \quad}$$

$$\underline{\quad 5 \quad} \quad \underline{\quad \text{2} \quad} \quad = \quad \underline{\qquad}$$

$$\underline{\quad 3 \quad} \text{ take away } \underline{\qquad} \text{ is } \underline{\qquad}$$

$$\underline{\quad 3 \quad} \quad - \quad \underline{\qquad} \quad = \quad \underline{\qquad}$$

$$\underline{\quad 4 \quad} \text{ take away } \underline{\qquad} \text{ is } \underline{\qquad}$$

$$\underline{\quad 4 \quad} \quad - \quad \underline{\qquad} \quad = \quad \underline{\qquad}$$

Skills: Recognizing sets of objects and writing corresponding numerals; Subtracting groups of objects; Understanding subtraction sentences

BASIC MATH SKILLS

Look at each picture.
How many are left?

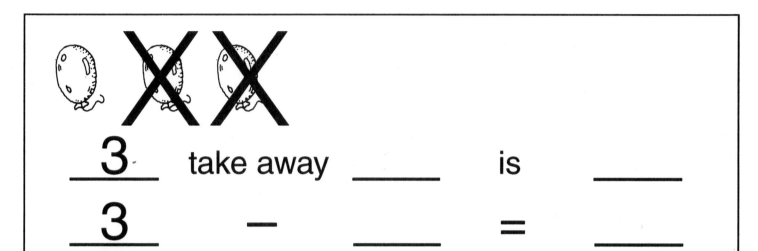

__3__ take away _____ is _____

__3__   –   _____ = _____

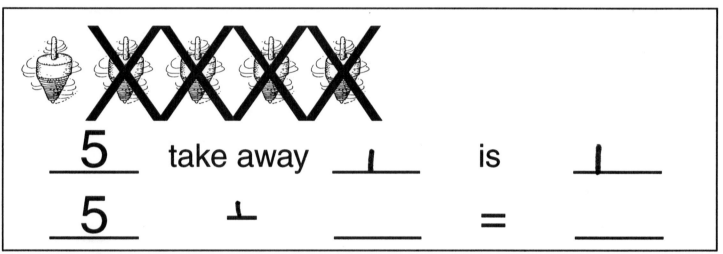

__5__ take away __⊥__ is __⊥__

__5__   ⊥   _____ = _____

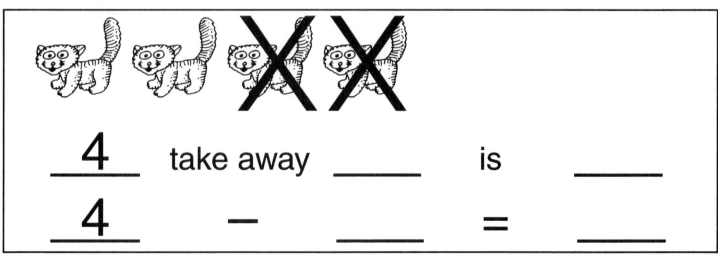

__4__ take away _____ is _____

__4__   –   _____ = _____

Skills: Recognizing sets of objects and writing corresponding numerals; Subtracting groups of objects; Understanding subtraction sentences

BASIC MATH SKILLS

Look at each picture.
How many are left?

5   –   1   =   ____

2   –   1   =   ____

3   –   2   =   ____

Skills: Recognizing sets of objects and writing corresponding numerals; Subtracting groups of objects; Understanding subtraction problems

BASIC MATH SKILLS

Look at each picture.
How many are left?

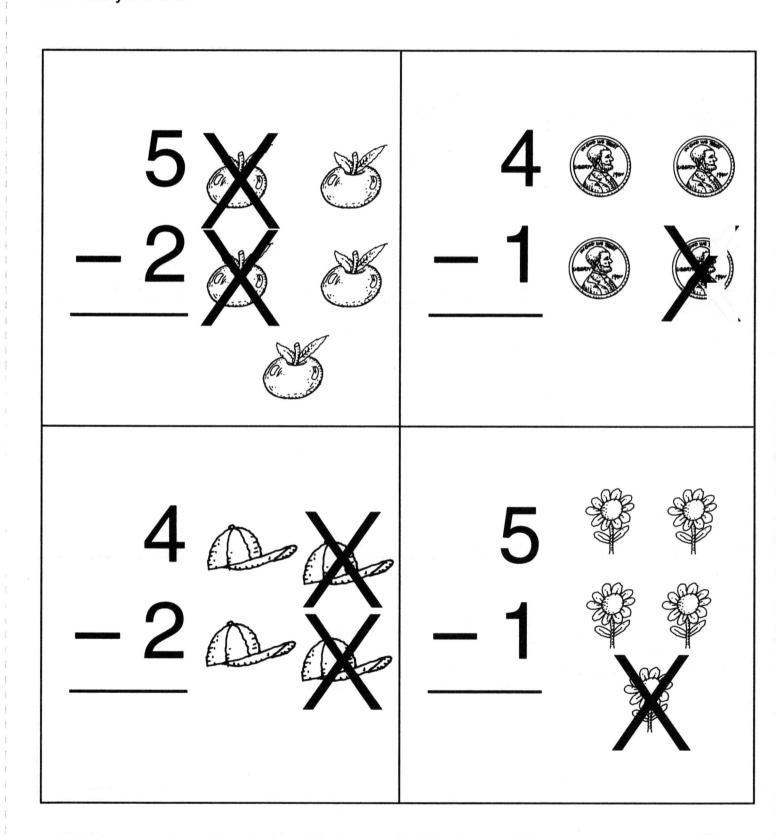

Skills: Solving vertical problems; Writing numerals

BASIC MATH SKILLS

Look at each picture.
How many are left?

$$
\begin{array}{r}
5 \\
-2 \\
\hline
\end{array}
$$

$$
\begin{array}{r}
4 \\
-1 \\
\hline
\end{array}
$$

$$
\begin{array}{r}
4 \\
-2 \\
\hline
\end{array}
$$

$$
\begin{array}{r}
5 \\
-1 \\
\hline
\end{array}
$$

Skills: Solving vertical problems; Writing numerals

BASIC MATH SKILLS

Subtract the numbers in each heart.
If the answer is **1**, color it red.
If the answer is **2**, color it yellow.
If the answer is **3**, color it green.

Skills: Solving vertical subtraction problems; Writing numerals

BASIC MATH SKILLS

How many are left?
Subtract to find out.

$$\begin{array}{r} 5 \\ -\ 2 \\ \hline \end{array}$$

$$\begin{array}{r} 3 \\ -\ 2 \\ \hline \end{array}$$

$$\begin{array}{r} 4 \\ -\ 3 \\ \hline \end{array}$$

$$\begin{array}{r} 4 \\ -\ 2 \\ \hline \end{array}$$

$$\begin{array}{r} 5 \\ -\ 4 \\ \hline \end{array}$$

Skills: Solving subtraction problems; Writing numerals

BASIC MATH SKILLS

Subtract. Then color each picture.

$$\begin{array}{r} 10 \\ -\ 7 \\ \hline \end{array}$$

$$\begin{array}{r} 9 \\ -\ 4 \\ \hline \end{array}$$

Skills: Solving subtraction problems; Writing numerals

BASIC MATH SKILLS

Follow the dots from **1** to **25** to find a furry friend.

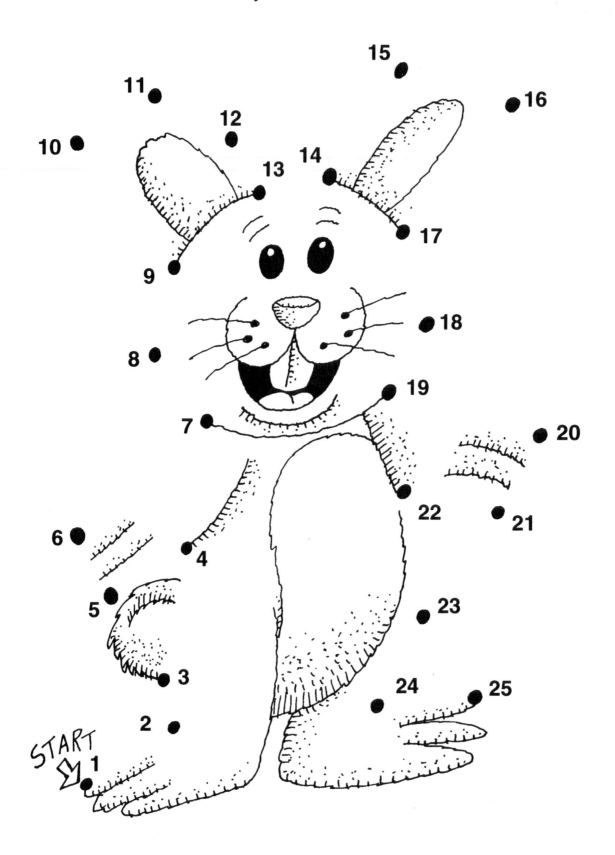

Skills: Order of numerals from one to twenty-five; Following directions

BASIC MATH SKILLS

Look at these footballs.
Make groups of **ten**.

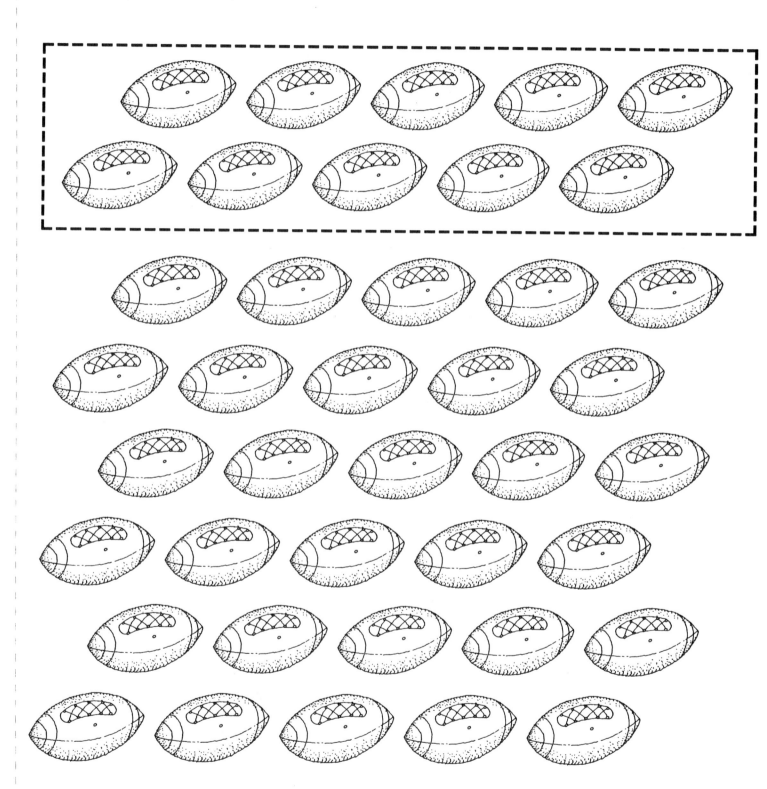

Skills: Forming groups of ten; Counting objects to form groups

BASIC MATH SKILLS

Watch the train race down the track.
How many circles do you see?
Put an **X** on each one.

Skills: Identifying circles; Counting

BASIC MATH SKILLS

Which path leads to the pond?
Is it the one with **squares** or the one with **circles**?
Find out by leading the duck to the pond.

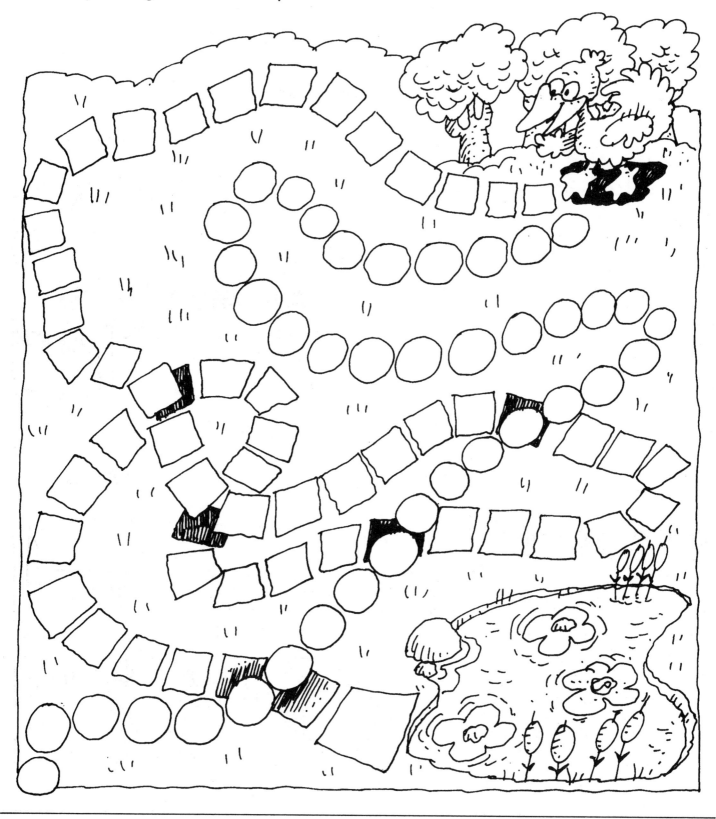

Skills: Identifying squares and circles

BASIC MATH SKILLS

Let's visit the farm.
How many triangles do you see?
Put an **X** on each one.

Skills: Identifying triangles; Counting

BASIC MATH SKILLS

The children are building a fortress.
Help them build it.
Color all the **rectangles** you see red.
Color the rest of the shapes blue.

Skills: Identifying rectangles

BASIC MATH SKILLS

Color all the **triangles** blue.
Color all the **circles** yellow.
Color all the **rectangles** green.
Color all the **squares** red.

Skills: Identifying shapes

BASIC MATH SKILLS

Trace each shape.
Draw shapes that look the same.
Use the dots to help you.
Then color and name each shape.

Skills: Recognizing shapes; Forming rectangles and squares

BASIC MATH SKILLS

Trace each shape.
Draw shapes that look the same.
Use the dots to help you.
Then color and name each shape.

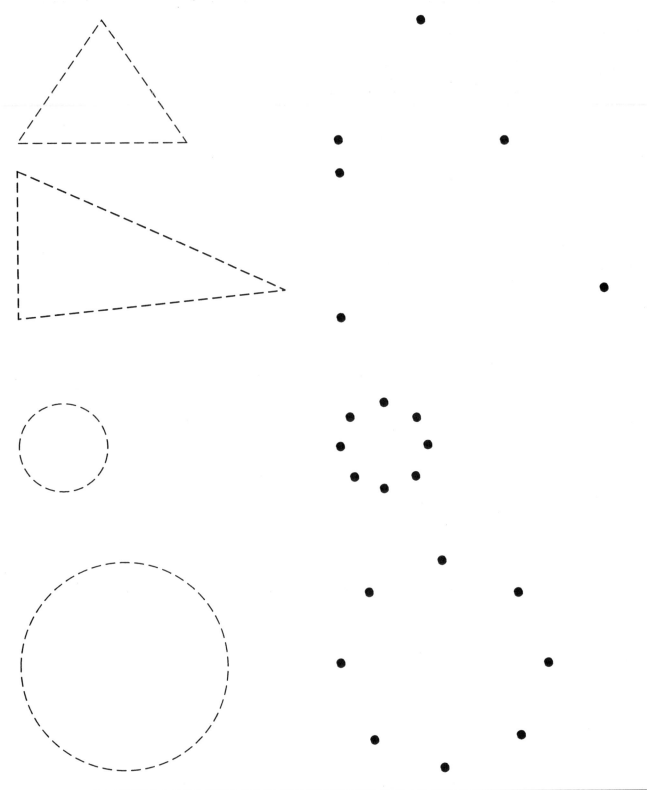

Skills: Recognizing shapes; Forming triangles and circles

BASIC MATH SKILLS

Let's find seashells!
Look at the pattern in each row.
Draw a circle around the shell that continues each pattern.

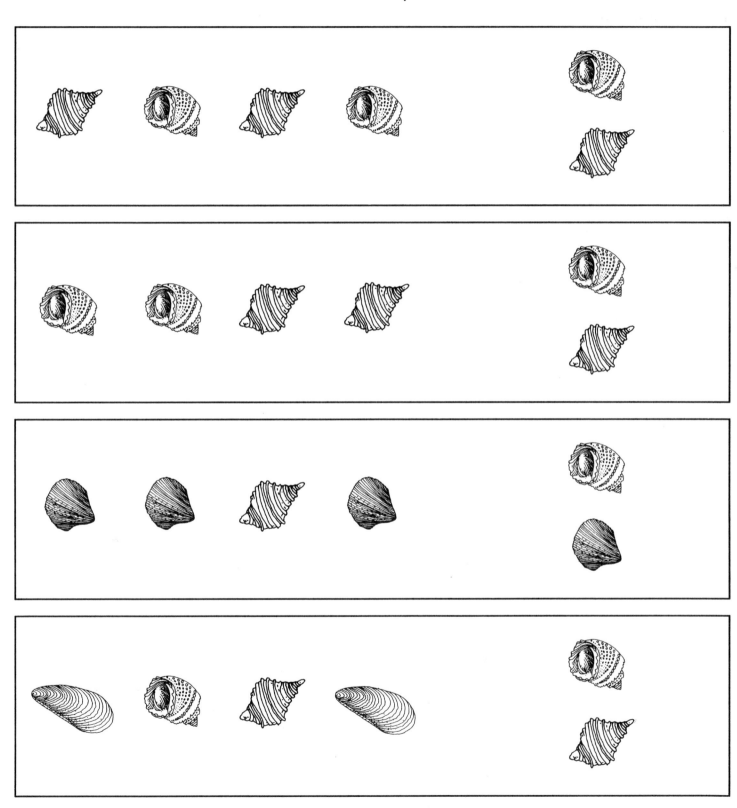

Skills: Observing and continuing patterns

BASIC MATH SKILLS

Look at the pattern in each row.
Draw shapes to continue each pattern.

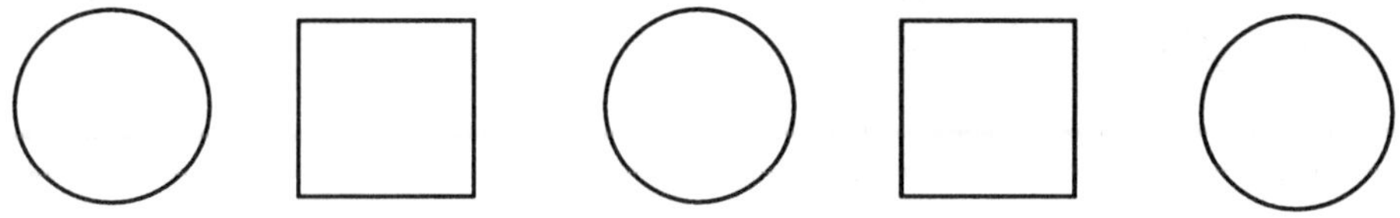

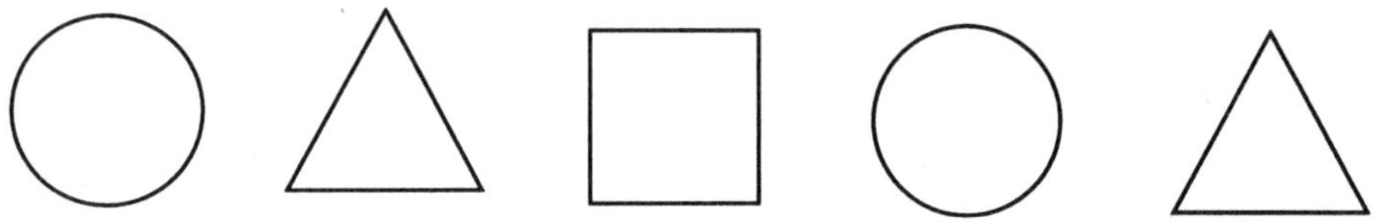

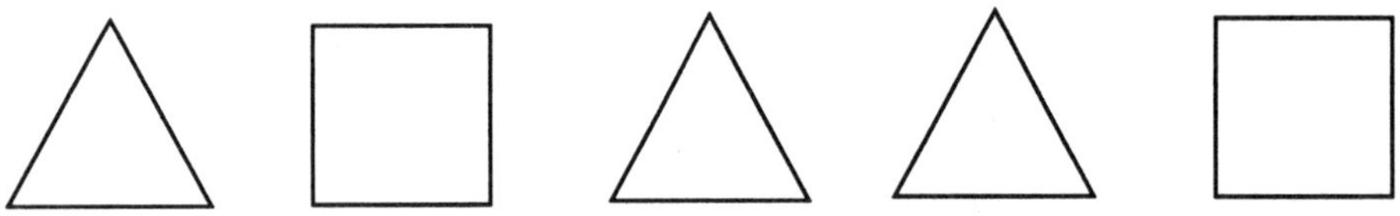

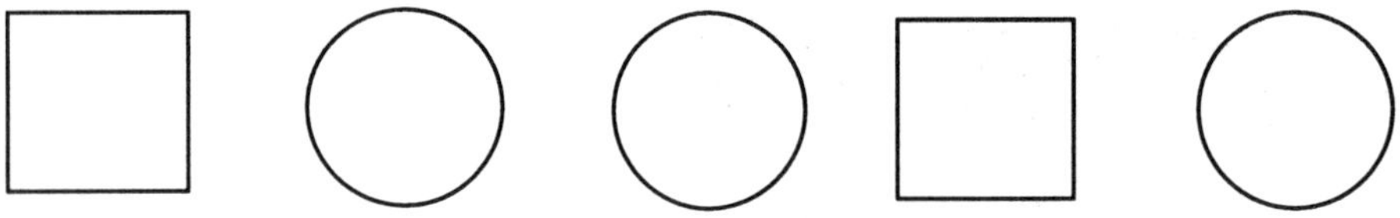

○ □ ○ □ ○

○ △ □ ○ △

△ □ △ △ □

□ ○ ○ □ ○

Skills: Observing and continuing patterns

BASIC MATH SKILLS

Let's play ball!
How many sports can you play?
Look at the pattern in each row.
Draw a circle around the picture that continues each pattern.

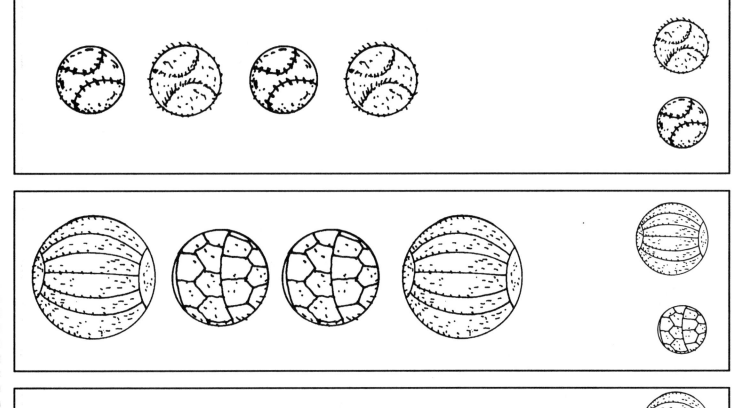

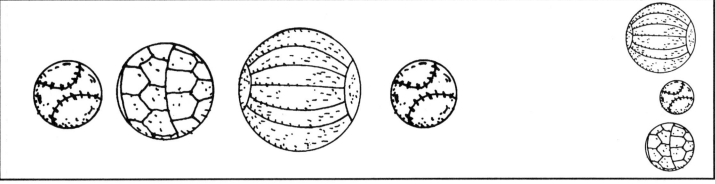

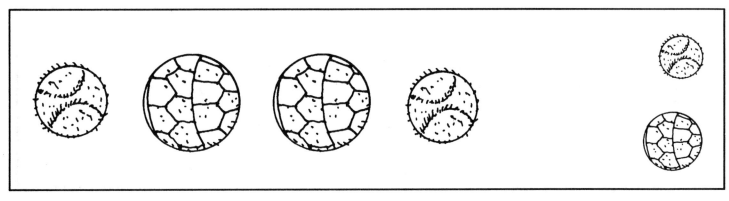

Skills: Observing and continuing patterns

BASIC MATH SKILLS

Every child wants a balloon.
Draw lines to connect each child with a balloon.

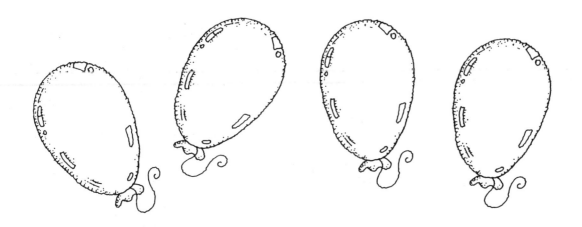

Skills: One-to-one correspondence; Matching

BASIC MATH SKILLS

Look at the first table.
Count the number in each set of cupcakes.
Then look at the second table.
Count the number in each set of cupcakes.
Then draw lines to connect the sets with the same number of foods.

Skills: Identifying sets; Matching

BASIC MATH SKILLS

Look at all the umbrellas!
Look at the dots on each umbrella at the right.
Find the shell on the left that matches it.
Draw lines to connect them.

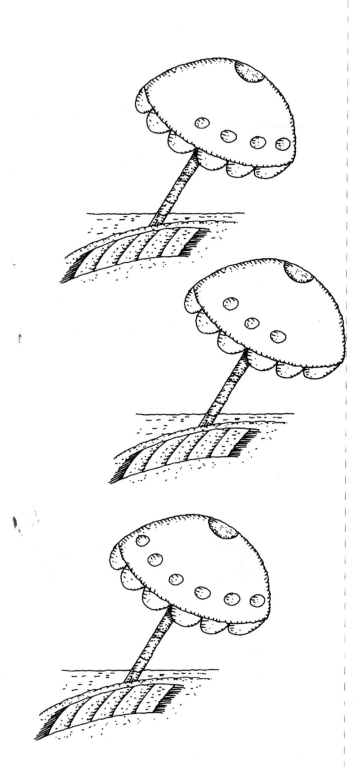

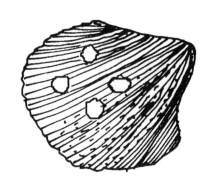

Skills: Identifying sets; Matching

BASIC MATH SKILLS

Look at the dots on the dominoes.
Color the one that shows fewer dots than the other domino.

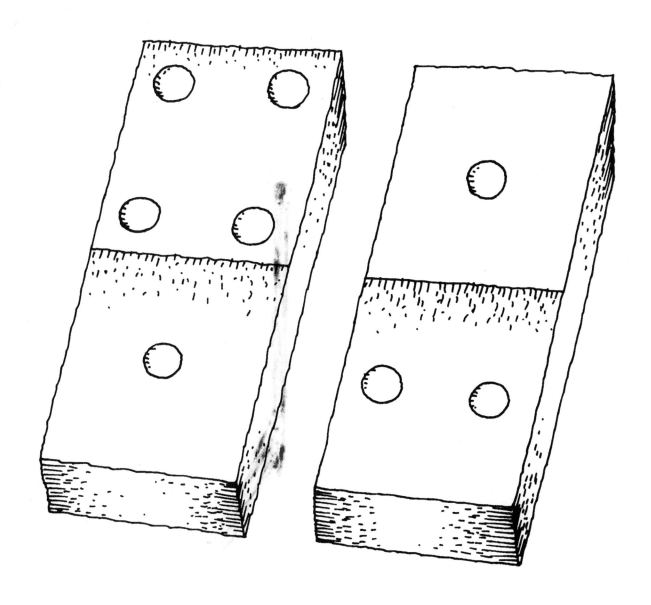

BASIC MATH SKILLS

The kitten got into the jam.
Look what he did to the chairs.
Color the chair that shows more paw prints than the other chair.

Skills: Identifying sets; Understanding more than

BASIC MATH SKILLS

Look at the dots inside each balloon.
Color the balloons that show 2 dots blue.
Color the balloons that show 4 dots green.
Color the balloons that show 6 dots yellow.
Color the balloons that show 8 dots orange.
Color the balloons that show 10 dots red.

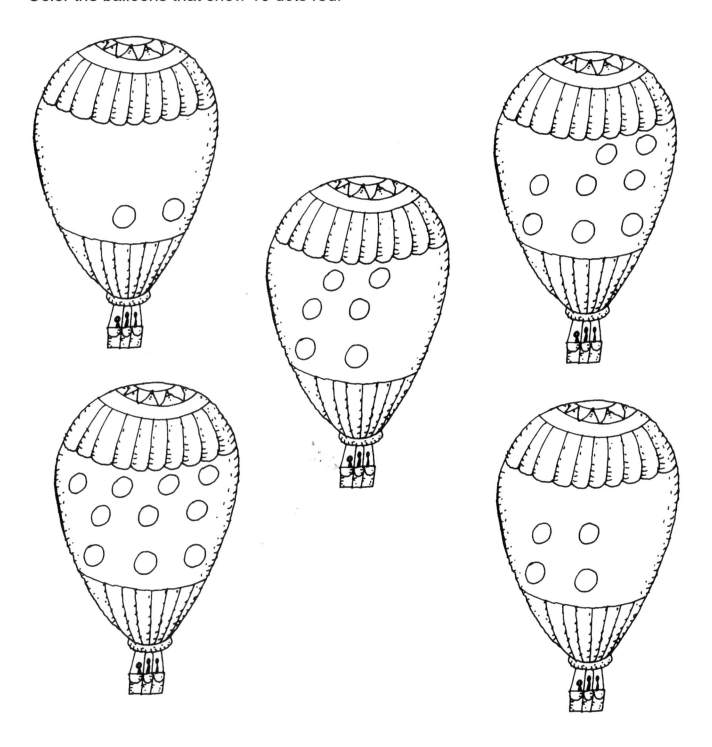

Skills: Counting; Identifying sets

BASIC MATH SKILLS

We need to get supplies for school!
Look at the numbers on the left.
Look at the supplies on the rest of the page.
Count the number of school supplies in each group.
Draw a line to connect each number with the correct number of supplies.

1

3

5

7

Skills: Counting; Identifying sets; Recognizing numbers

BASIC MATH SKILLS

Let's go to the supermarket.
Look at each number and the picture next to it on the grocery list.
Circle that number of things at the supermarket.

kills: Creating sets of objects; Recognizing numbers; Counting

BASIC MATH SKILLS

Let's have a party!
Look at each number and the picture next to it on the party list.
Circle that number of things at the party store.

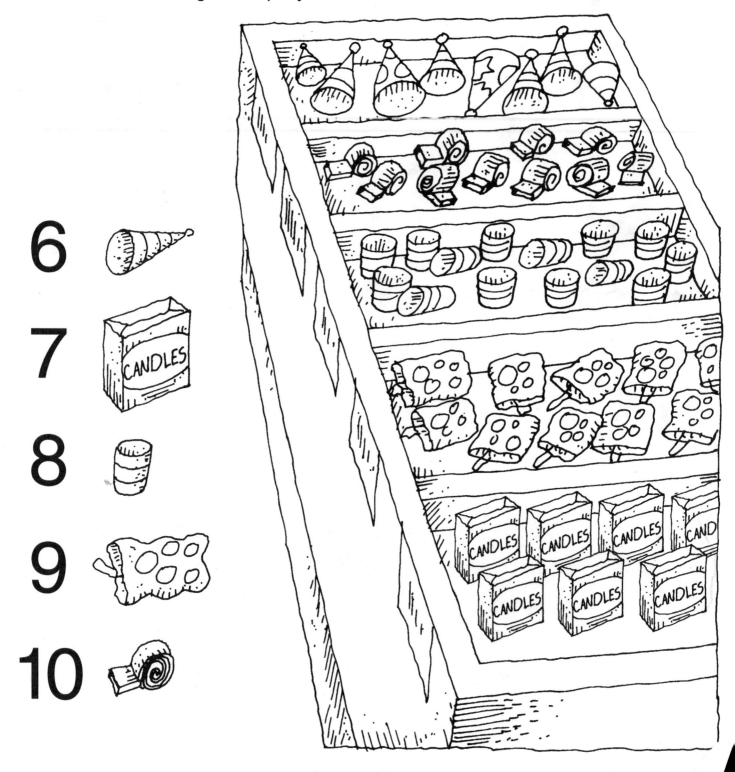

6

7 CANDLES

8

9

10

Skills: Creating sets of objects; Recognizing numbers; Counting

BASIC MATH SKILLS

Where is the sea lion?
Follow the dots from **1** to **50** to find out.
Then finish coloring the picture.

Skills: Number order; Recognizing numbers

BASIC MATH SKILLS

Watch the farmer bring in his crop!
Use the color code to finish the picture.

Color: 1 = red   2 = orange   7 = brown
        3 = green   4 = yellow
        5 = blue   6 = black

Skills: Recognizing numbers; Matching numbers to color codes

BASIC MATH SKILLS

The kittens are having fun!
Use the color code to finish the picture.

Color: 1 = red   2 = blue   7 = orange
        3 = green   4 = yellow
        5 = black   6 = brown

Skills: Recognizing numbers; Matching numbers to color codes

BASIC MATH SKILLS

Let's go to the playground!
Follow the numbers down the path to get to the playground.
Begin at 1.
Trace each number.

Skills: Recognizing numbers; Writing numbers

BASIC MATH SKILLS

How many cupcakes did we make?
Count them.
Write one number on each cupcake, from **1** to **12**.

Skills: Counting; Writing numbers from 1 to 12

BASIC MATH SKILLS

Look at the train.
Circle the **first** car.
Draw a **line** under the **second** car.
Put an **X** on the **third** car.

Skills: Recognizing ordinal numbers; Developing vocabulary

BASIC MATH SKILLS

What a long chain of flowers!
Color the **first**, **second** and **third** flowers blue.
Color the **fourth**, **fifth** and **sixth** flowers red.
Color the **seventh**, **eighth** and **ninth** flowers green.
Color the **tenth** flower any color you wish.

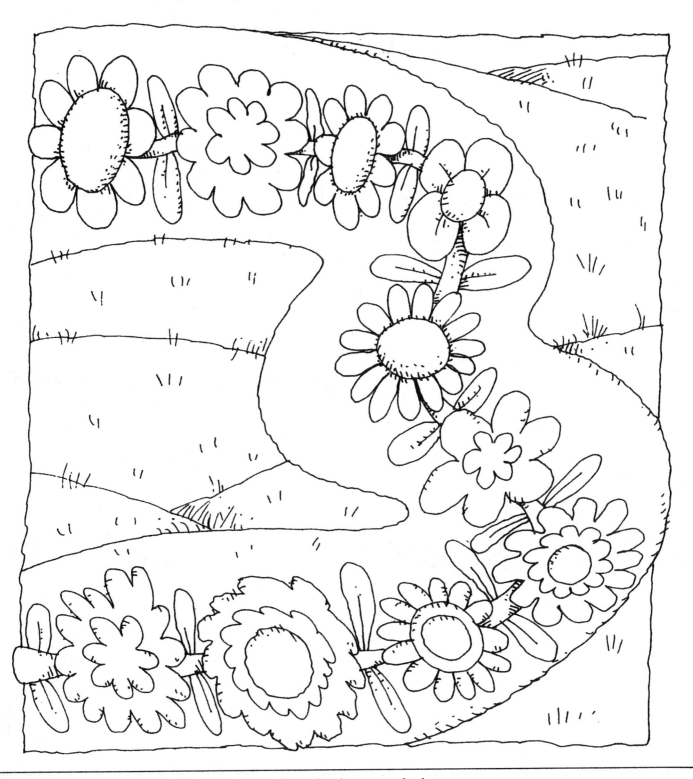

Skills: Recognizing ordinal numbers; Developing vocabulary

BASIC MATH SKILLS

What fun!
Find and circle the numbers **1** through **10** hidden in this picture.

Skills: Counting; Recognizing numerals

BASIC MATH SKILLS

Drive the cart through the course and look for numbers.
Find and circle the numbers **1** through **10** hidden in this picture.

Skills: Counting; Recognizing numerals

BASIC MATH SKILLS

Play teddy bear bingo with a friend.
Use the teddy bear on this page.
Your friend can use the one on the
following page.

You'll need: 1 pair of dice

The first player rolls the dice and covers the number rolled on his teddy bear.
Then the second player rolls and covers the number rolled on her teddy bear.
If a number is already covered, you skip a turn.
The winner is the player who covers all his teddy bear's numbers first.

Skills: Counting; Matching; Identifying numbers to 10

BASIC MATH SKILLS

Use this teddy bear
to play teddy bear bingo.

Skills: Counting; Matching; Identifying numbers to 10

BASIC MATH SKILLS

Look at the numbers on the cupcakes.
Write the missing numbers.

Skills: Ordering numbers; Writing numbers

BASIC MATH SKILLS

Play Sack Race.
Toss the penny.
If it lands on heads, trace number 1 under the girl racer.
If it lands on tails, trace number 1 under the boy racer.
Keep tossing the penny and tracing the number under either the boy or girl.
See which child gets to the finish line first.

You'll need: 1penny

Finish line

1 2 3 4 5 6 7 8 9 10

1 2 3 4 5 6 7 8 9 10

Skills: Counting; Identifying and writing numbers to 10; Probability

BASIC MATH SKILLS

Play the sack race again.
Only this time, trace the numbers **11-20**.
See page 139 for directions.

**Finish
line**

11 12 13 14 15 16 17 18 19 20

11 12 13 14 15 16 17 18 19 20

Skills: Counting; Identifying and writing numbers 11-20; Probability

BASIC MATH SKILLS

Here comes the mail carrier!
He needs to put the **small** packages in the **top** sack
and the **large** packages in the **bottom** sack.
Draw lines to connect each package to its right sack.

Skills: Developing vocabulary; Making comparisons

BASIC MATH SKILLS

We're picking apples!
Look at the pairs of apples below.
Circle the **smaller** apples.
Draw a line under the **larger** apples.

Skills: Developing vocabulary; Making comparisons

BASIC MATH SKILLS

Look at each group of animals.
Circle the **smallest** one in each group.
Put an **X** on the **largest** one in each group

Skills: Developing vocabulary; Making comparisons

BASIC MATH SKILLS

Look at the numbers on the turtle's back.
Color all the numbers that are **greater than** 5 blue.
Color all the numbers that are **less than** 5 red.

Skills: Recognizing numbers; Understanding greater than and less than; Making comparisons

BASIC MATH SKILLS

Look what the fisherman caught!
Look at the numbers in each pair of fish.
Color the fish with the **greater** number **orange**.
Color the fish with the **lesser** number **yellow**.

Skills: Recognizing numbers; Understanding greater than and less than

BASIC MATH SKILLS

Look at the pairs of things around the island and in the sea.
Circle the **lighter** one.
Put an **X** on the **heavier** one.

Skills: Developing vocabulary; Comparing weight; Thinking critically

146

BASIC MATH SKILLS

Look at the pairs of things in the kitchen.
Circle the **lighter** one.
Put an **X** on the **heavier** one.

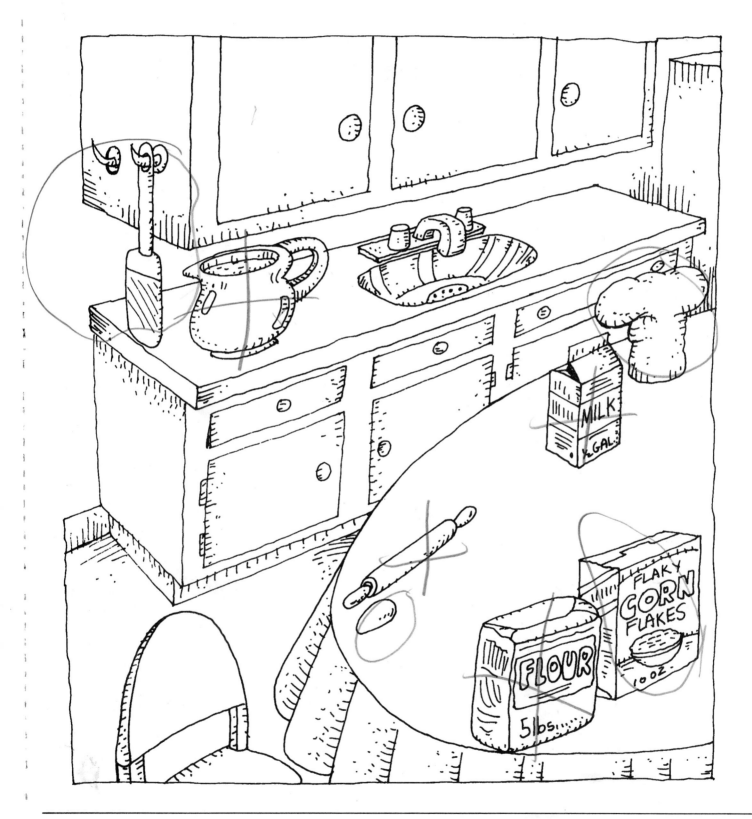

Skills: Developing vocabulary; Comparing weight; Thinking critically

BASIC MATH SKILLS

Find pairs that are alike except for their height.
Circle the **shorter** one.
Put an **X** on the **taller** one.

Skills: Developing vocabulary; Comparing height

BASIC MATH SKILLS

Look at the elephants on parade.
Circle the **shorter** one in each pair.

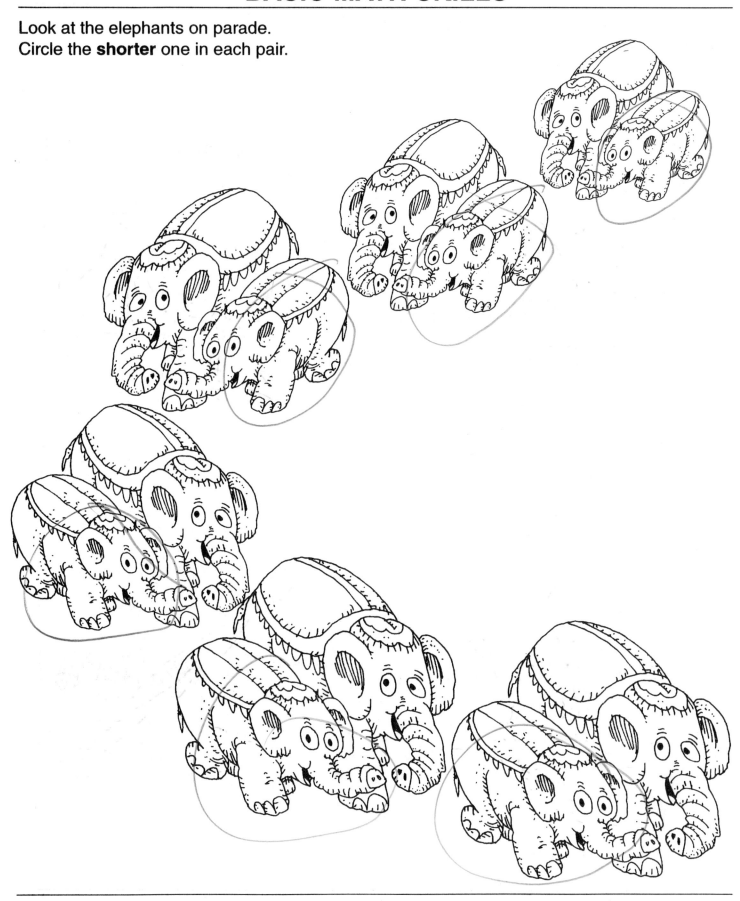

Skills: Developing vocabulary; Comparing height

BASIC MATH SKILLS

Everyone is going to the carousel.
Which path should they take?
Look at each set of paths.
Trace the path that is **shorter**.
Cross out the path that is **longer**.

Skills: Developing vocabulary; Comparing length

BASIC MATH SKILLS

Look what is inside the toy chests!
Look at the toys next to each child.
Circle the one that is **shorter**.
Put an X on the one that is **longer**.

Skills: Developing vocabulary; Comparing length

BASIC MATH SKILLS

The fishermen are using a fish to measure.
Help them find out the length of each object.
Look at the pictures.
Count how many fish lengths long it is.
Then write the number on the line.

Measuring fish

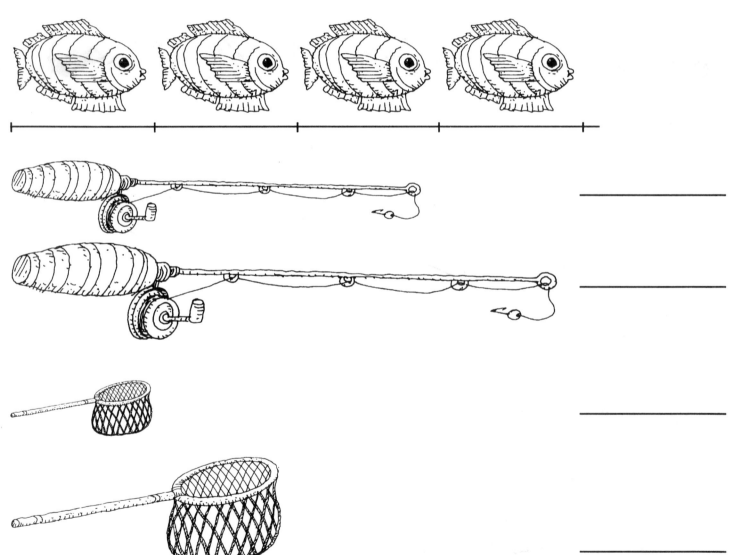

_____

_____

_____

_____

Skills: Measuring length; Counting; Writing numbers

BASIC MATH SKILLS

The bear is using his paw prints to measure.
Help him find out the length of each object.
Look at the pictures.
Count how many paw prints long it is.
Then write the number on the line.

Measuring paws

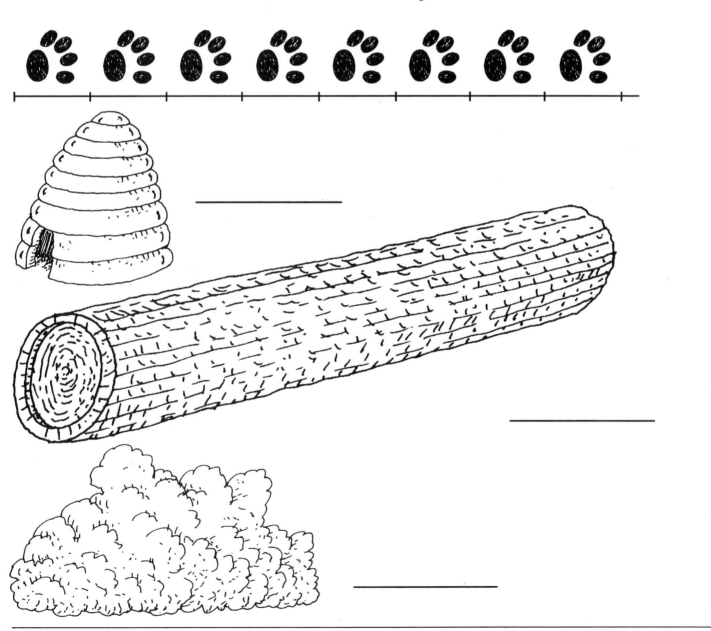

Skills: Measuring length; Counting; Writing numbers

BASIC MATH SKILLS

The farmer is measuring his squash.
Help him find the length of each squash.
Look at each one.
Count and trace the numbers to show how many squares long it is.
Then write the number on the line.

1	2	3	4	5

_____

_____

_____

Skills: Measuring length; Counting; Writing numbers

BASIC MATH SKILLS

Will the dolls fit in my doll bed?
Use the ruler to find out the length of each doll.
Look at the doll in each box.
Count the numbers to show how long it is.
Then write the number on the line.

——————————   ——————————   ——————————

Skills: Measuring length; Counting; Writing numbers

TIME AND MONEY

Look at the pictures in each box.
Circle the picture that shows which
activity takes more time to do.

Skills: Time awareness; Identifying which takes more time

156

TIME AND MONEY

Look at the pictures in each box.
Circle the picture that shows which
activity takes less time to do.

Skills: Time awareness; Identifying which takes less time

TIME AND MONEY

What time is it?
Look at each clock.
Write the time.

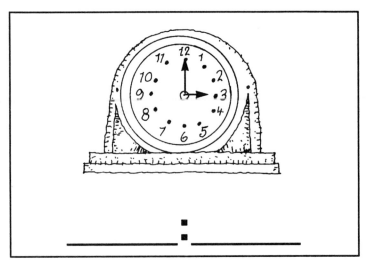

_____ : _____

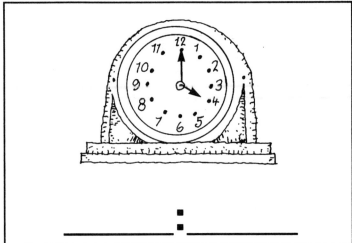

_____ : _____

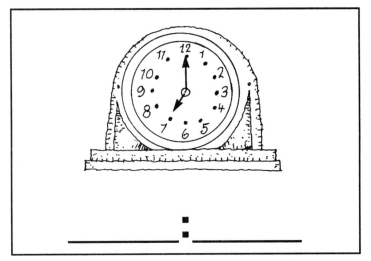

_____ : _____

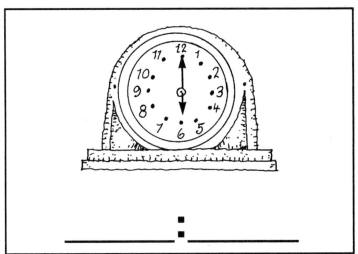

_____ : _____

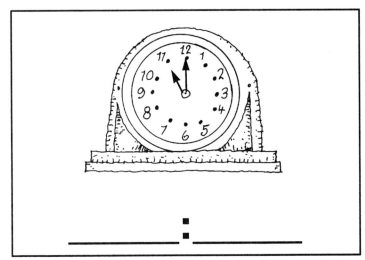

_____ : _____

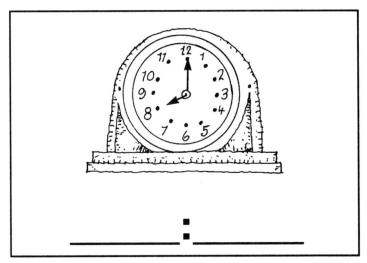

_____ : _____

Skills: Time awareness; Telling time to the hour

TIME AND MONEY

Tell me the time.
Look at each clock.
Write the time.

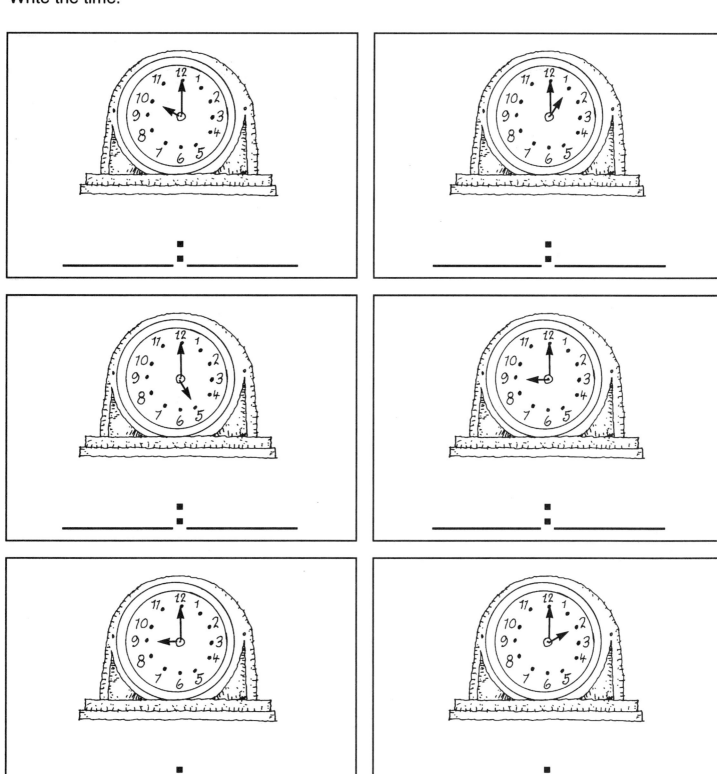

Skills: Time awareness; Telling time to the hour

TIME AND MONEY

Put the time on the clock!
Look at the time.
Draw the hands on each clock to show the correct time.

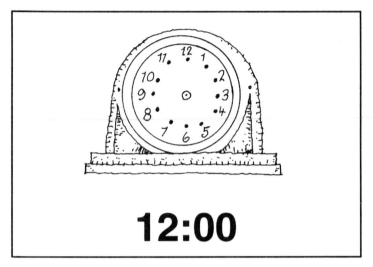

12:00

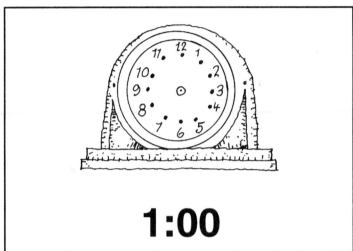

1:00

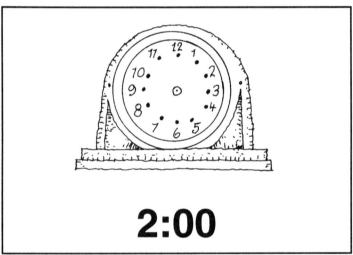

2:00

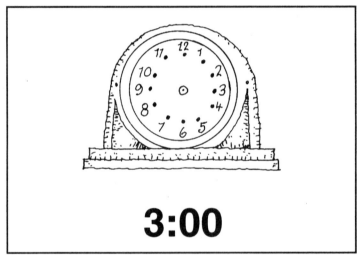

3:00

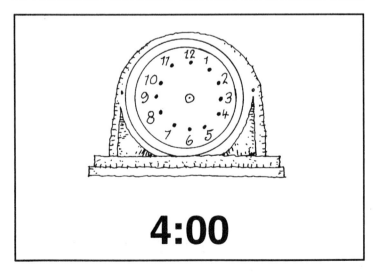

4:00

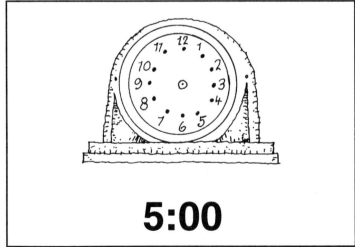

5:00

Skills: Time awareness; Showing time to the hour

TIME AND MONEY

Show the time on the clock!
Look at the time.
Draw the hands on each clock to show the correct time.

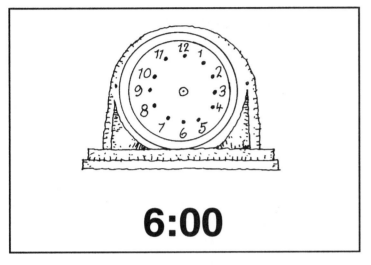

6:00

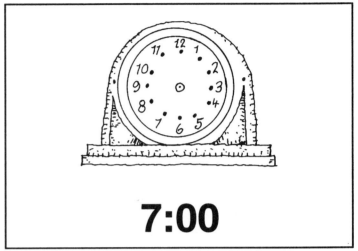

7:00

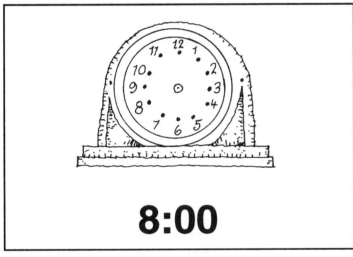

8:00

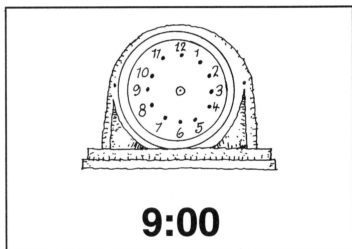

9:00

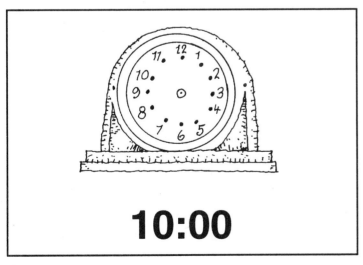

10:00

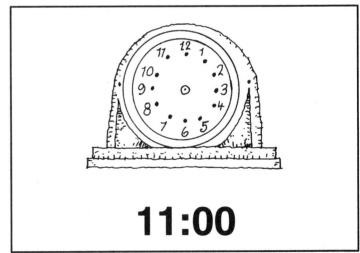

11:00

Skills: Time awareness; Showing time to the hour

TIME AND MONEY

Can I buy it?
A penny is worth one cent.
Put an **X** on the coins you need to buy each candy.

 1¢

 2¢

 3¢

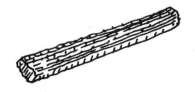 4¢

Skills: Money awareness; Understanding the value of a penny

TIME AND MONEY

Can I buy it?
A nickel is worth five cents.
A nickel is the same as five pennies.
Put an **X** on the coins you need to buy each toy.

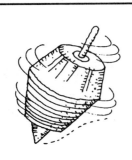 5¢

 8¢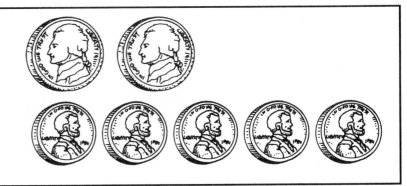

 7¢

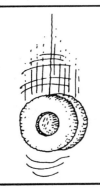 10¢

Skills: Money awareness; Understanding the value of a penny and a nickel

TIME AND MONEY

Can I buy it?
A dime is worth ten cents.
A dime is the same as ten pennies or two nickels.
Put an **X** on the coins you need to buy each toy.

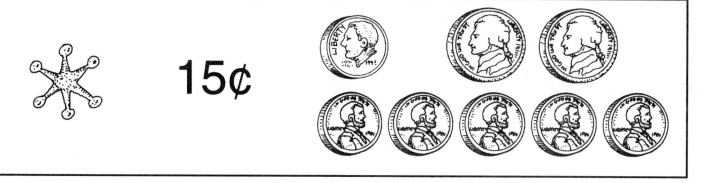

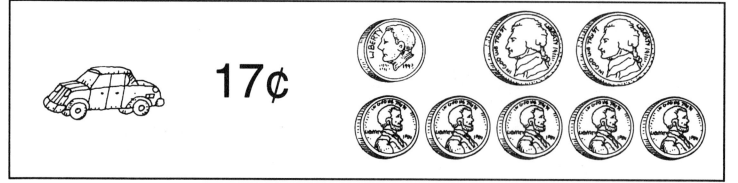

Skills: Money awareness; Understanding the value of a penny, a nickel, and a dime

TIME AND MONEY

How much does it cost?
How much money is needed to buy each item?
Draw a line to show the the money that matches each price tag.

10¢

17¢

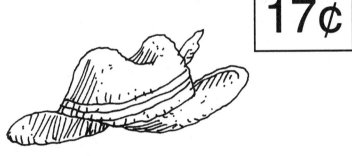

20¢

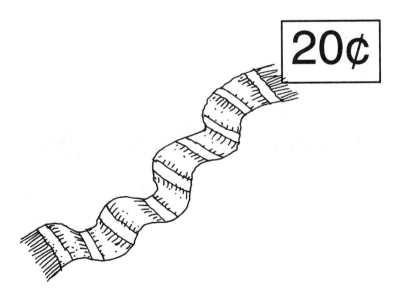

Skills: Money awareness; Understanding the value of a penny, a nickel, and a dime

READING READINESS

Look at the cookies we baked!
Look at the letters in each cookie.
Color the cookies with lower case letters one color.
Color the cookies with upper case letters another color.
Then finish coloring the picture.

Skills: Distinguishing upper and lower case letters; Recognizing letters; Developing fine motor skills

READING READINESS

Look at each picture.
Draw a line between the things that are the same.

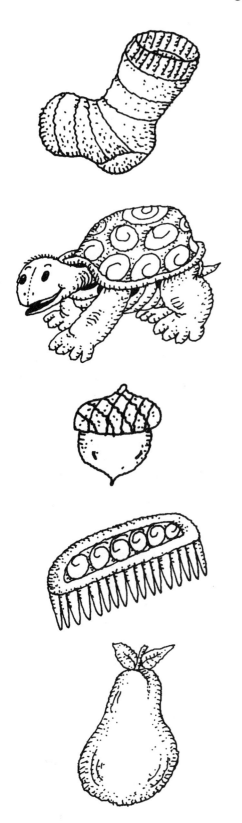
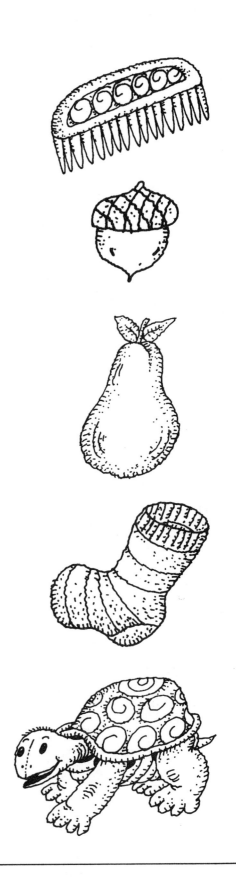

Skills: Visual matching; Classification

READING READINESS

Color the two pictures in each box that go together.

Skills: Association; Classification; Logical reasoning

READING READINESS

Look at the pictures in each row.
Cross out the one that is different.
Then color the others.

Skills: Visual discrimination; Noticing details

READING READINESS

Which one does not belong?
Cross out the one that does not belong with the others.
Then color the other pictures.

Skills: Classification; Association

READING READINESS

Look closely at each row of pictures.
One of the objects is in a different position.
Cross it out and then color the other pictures.

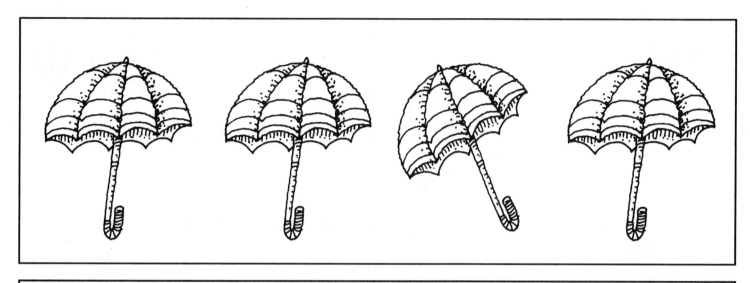

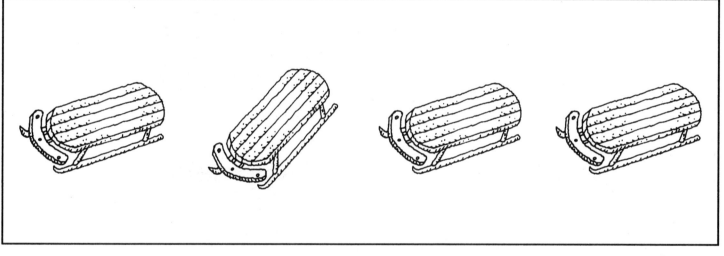

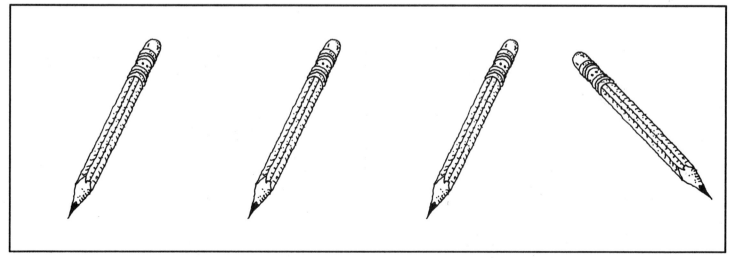

Skills: Visual discrimination; Noticing details; Spatial orientation

READING READINESS

Look at the large pictures.
Then look at the detail in each small box.

Find the detail in each large picture and circle it.
Then color the pictures.

Skills: Visual discrimination; Noticing details

READING READINESS

Look at the pictures in each box.
Circle the pictures that are facing right.
Make an "X" over the pictures that are facing left.

Skills: Recognizing right and left

READING READINESS

Look at the first picture in each row and say its name.
Circle the picture whose name rhymes with it.

Skills: Auditory discrimination; Reproducing sounds

READING READINESS

Look at each picture.
Draw a line between the pictures whose names rhyme.

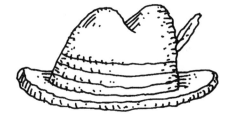

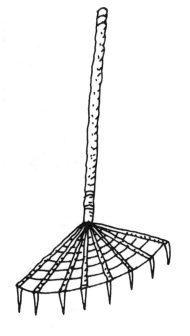

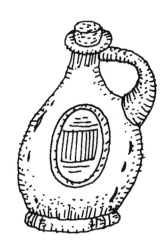

Skills: Auditory discrimination; Reproducing sounds

READING READINESS

Look at the pattern in each row.
Draw a line to the picture that continues each pattern.

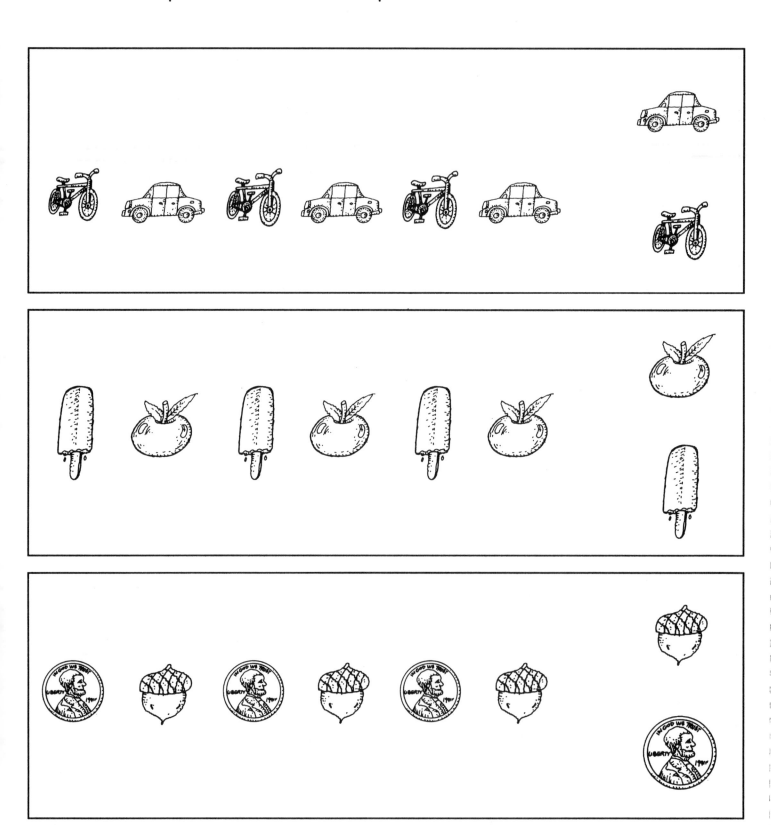

Skills: Observing and continuing patterns; Visual memory

READING READINESS

Look at the pattern in each row.
Draw a line to the picture that continues each pattern.

Skills: Observing and continuing patterns; Visual memory

READING READINESS

Look at the pattern in each row.
Draw a line to the picture that continues each pattern.

READING READINESS

Look at the pattern in each row.
Draw a line to the picture that continues each pattern.
Then color the shapes.

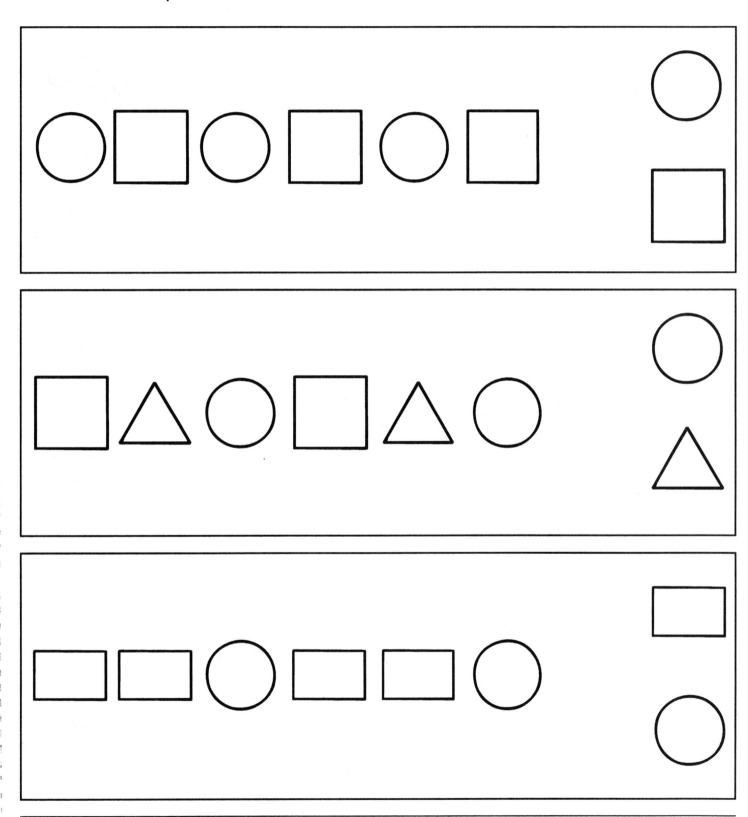

Skills: Observing and reproducing patterns; Visual memory; Fine motor skill development

READING READINESS

Look at the puppies.
Which ones are the same?
Draw lines to connect the ones that are alike.

Skills: Matching; Recognizing similarities

READING READINESS

The princess lost her slipper.
Help her find it.
Look at the slippers on this page.
Draw lines to connect the ones that are alike.
The one that does not have a match belongs to the princess.
Circle the princess's missing slipper.

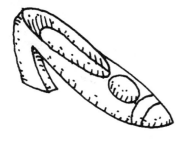

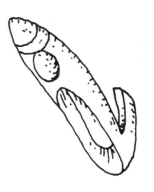

Skills: Matching; Recognizing similarities

READING READINESS

The animals are heading back to the farm.
Draw a line to connect each animal with its shadow.

Skills: Matching; Recognizing similarities

READING READINESS

They're coming around the mountain!
Draw a line to connect each vehicle with its shadow.

Skills: Matching; Recognizing similarities

READING READINESS

Look at the picture at the beginning of each row.
Then look at the other pictures in that row.
One picture is the same as the first one, but turned another way.
Find and circle that picture.

Skills: Noticing details; Recognizing differences

READING READINESS

Look at the picture at the beginning of each row.

Then look at the other pictures in that row.

One picture is the same as the first one, but turned another way.

Find and circle that picture.

Skills: Noticing details; Recognizing differences

READING READINESS

Look at the girl's ring.
Then look at the stones below.
Circle the one that is exactly like the stone in the girl's ring.

Skills: Noticing details; Recognizing differences

READING READINESS

Let's play dress-up.
Look at the girls on this page.
Find and circle the one that looks different.
Then color the rest of the picture.

Skills: Noticing details; Recognizing differences

READING READINESS

Help match the jewelry.
Look at each group of jewelry.
Circle the pieces that have the same shape.

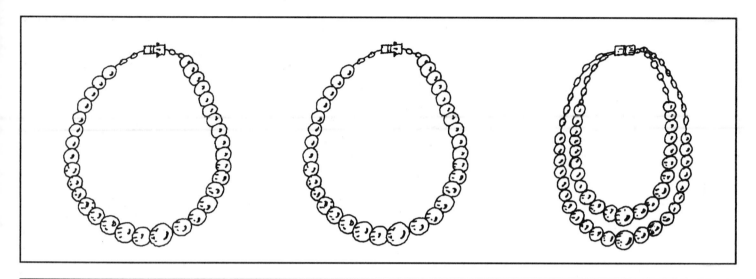

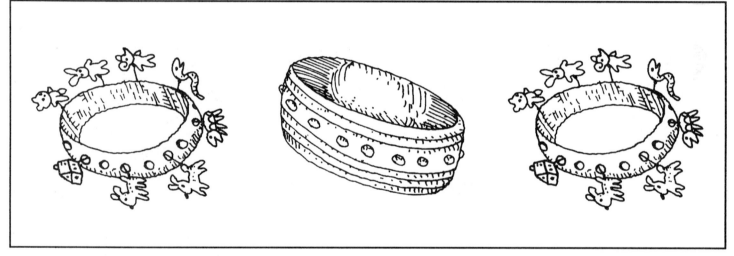

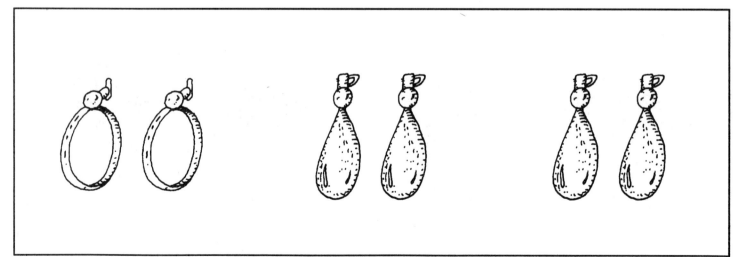

Skills: Noticing details; Recognizing differences; Identifying different attributes

READING READINESS

Help match the pictures.
Look at each group of drawings.
Circle the pictures that are the same.

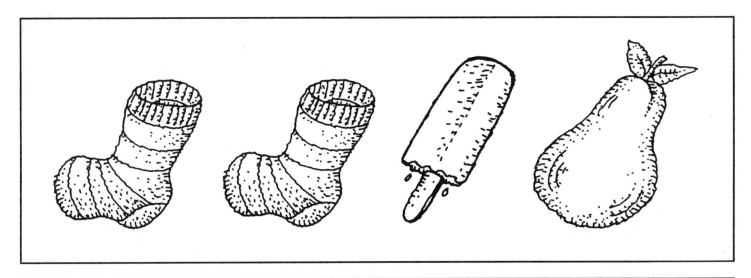

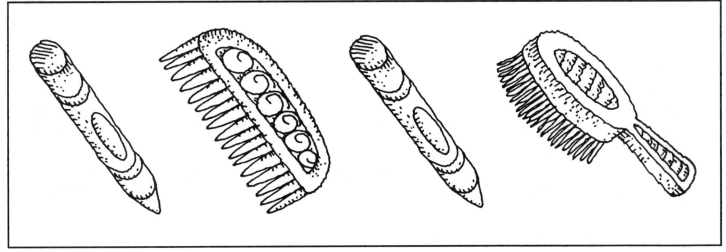

Skills: Recognizing similarities and differences; Identifying different attributes

READING READINESS

Work the puzzle!
Look at the finished puzzle.
Look at the loose pieces.
Draw lines to connect each puzzle piece to its
match in the completed puzzle.

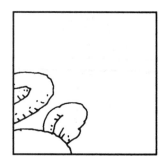
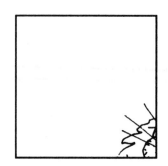

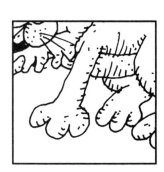
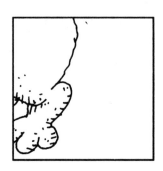

Skills: Spatial awareness; Visual perception; Developing fine motor skills

READING READINESS

Look at the finished puzzle.

Look at the loose pieces.

Draw lines to connect each puzzle piece to its match in the completed puzzle.

Skills: Spatial awareness; Visual perception; Developing fine motor skills

READING READINESS

Look at the picture.
Then look at the puzzle pieces.
Number the pieces, in order, from top to bottom.

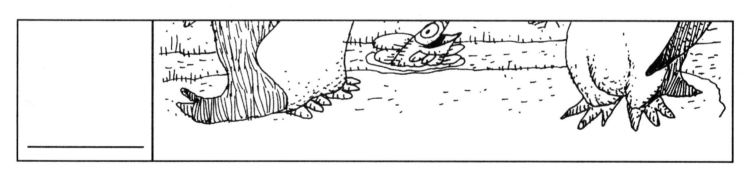

Skills: Spatial awareness; Visual perception; Developing fine motor skills

READING READINESS

Look at the monkey.
Then look at the puzzle pieces.
Number the pieces, in order, from top to bottom.

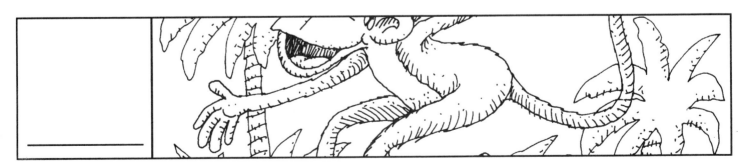

Skills: Spatial awareness; Visual perception; Developing fine motor skills

READING READINESS

Some pieces are missing from the circus puzzle.
Look at the number under each puzzle piece.
Find where that piece belongs in the puzzle.
Write its number on the line.

1   **2**   **3**

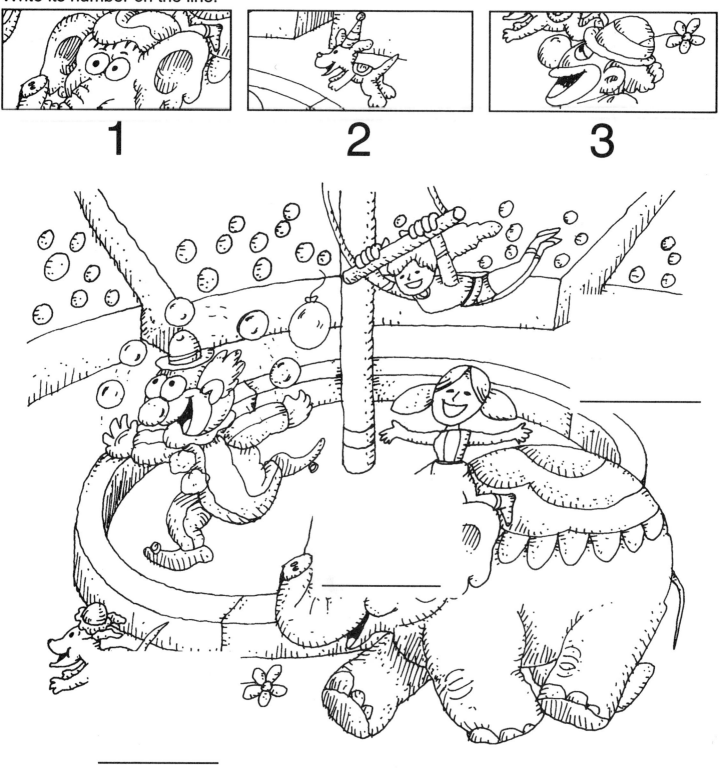

Skills: Visual perception; Deductive reasoning; Developing fine motor skills

READING READINESS

Look at the detail in each small box.
Find that detail in the picture below and circle it.

1

2

3

Skills: Noticing details

READING READINESS

Let's climb and jump and slide!
Look at the detail in each small box.
Find that detail in the picture below and circle it.

1
2
3

Skills: Noticing details

READING READINESS

The ship is ready to sail.
But some strange things have been stored on board.
Look at each object in the box.
Then find and circle each one in the picture below.

Skills: Visual perception; Visual memory

READING READINESS

School is fun.
But there are things that do not belong in the classroom.
Find and circle each.

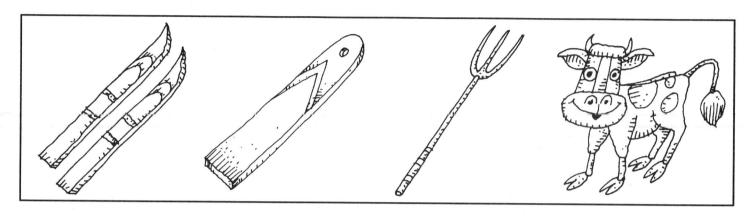

Skills: Thinking logically; Visual perception; Visual memory

READING READINESS

Dancing is such fun!
Look closely at both pictures.
Then circle five things that are at the top of the page
that are missing from the picture at the bottom.

Skills: Noticing details; Recognizing differences; Visual memory

READING READINESS

Let's color and paint today!
Look at both pictures.
Then circle five things at the top of the page that
are missing from the picture at the bottom.

Skills: Noticing details; Recognizing differences; Visual memory

READING READINESS

Sailing, sailing...
Look at both pictures.
Then circle five things at the top of the page that
are missing from the picture at the bottom.

Skills: Noticing details; Recognizing differences; Visual memory

READING READINESS

Mother and father are getting ready for a party.
But some things are very wrong.
Circle all the things that are wrong in the picture.

READING READINESS

The family is getting ready for dinner.
But some things are very wrong.
Circle all the things that are wrong in the picture.

Skills: Noticing details; Recognizing differences; Thinking logically

READING READINESS

What's for breakfast?
Find and circle the hidden letters.
Write each letter on the dashed lines below.
Then unscramble the letters to see what's for breakfast.

_____ _____ _____ _____ _____ _____ _____

Skills: Recognizing letters; Matching; Vocabulary

READING READINESS

What are the detectives looking for?
Find and circle the hidden letters.
Write each letter on the dashed lines below.
Then unscramble the letters to see what the detectives are looking for.

_____ _____ _____ _____ _____ _____

Skills: Recognizing letters; Vocabulary

READING READINESS

What are the children building?
Find and circle the hidden letters.
Write each letter on the dashed lines below.
Then unscramble the letters to see what the children are building.

_____ _____ _____ _____ _____

Skills: Recognizing letters; Vocabulary

READING READINESS

Toys, toys are everywhere!
Look carefully at all the toys.
When you are ready, turn the page to play a memory game.

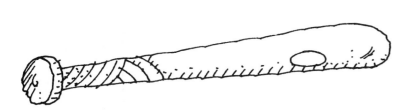

Skills: Visual memory; Association; Thinking logically

READING READINESS

Look at the pictures on this page.
Which ones do you remember from page 207?
Circle the ones you remember.

Skills: Thinking logically

READING READINESS

Look at the sets of objects on the left
Then find an object on the right that belongs to each set.
Draw lines to connect them.

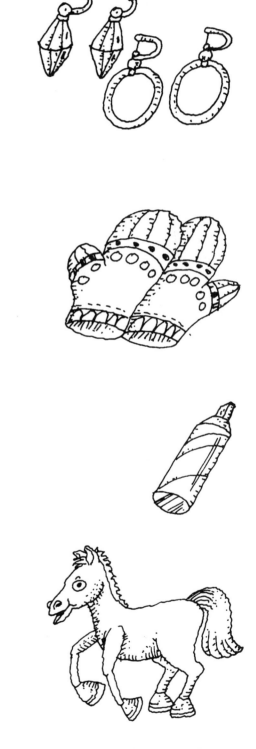

Skills: Classifying; Thinking logically

READING READINESS

Draw lines to connect each wheel to its vehicle.

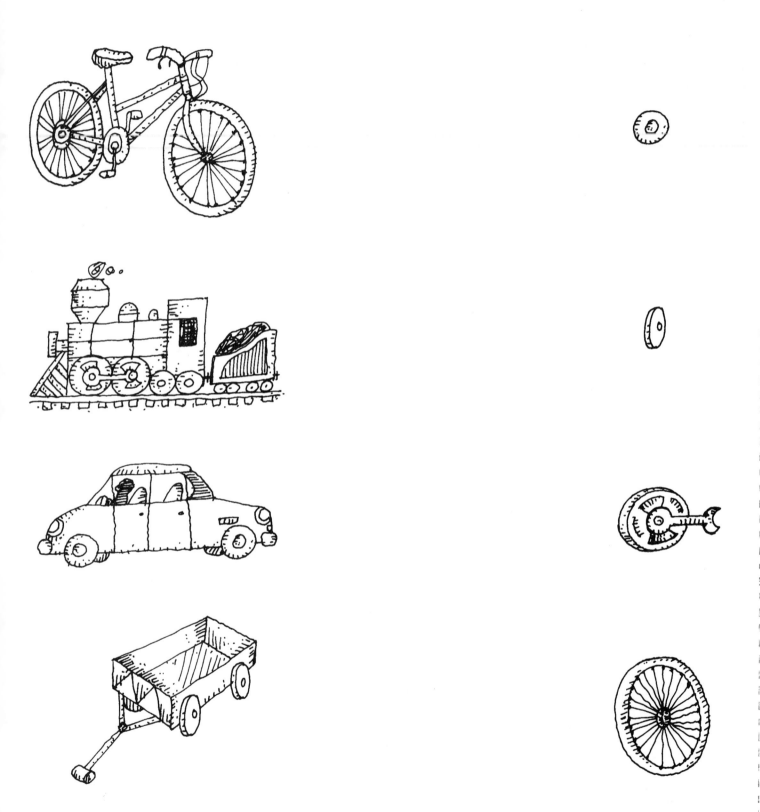

Skills: Classifying; Thinking logically; Visual matching

READING READINESS

Home, sweet home!
Look at each object at the top of the page.
Look at each room of the house.
Decide where each object belongs.
Then write its number in the correct box below.

1   2   3   4

READING READINESS

We need to sort the laundry!
Look at the clothes and the baskets below.
Draw lines to sort them into the correct baskets.

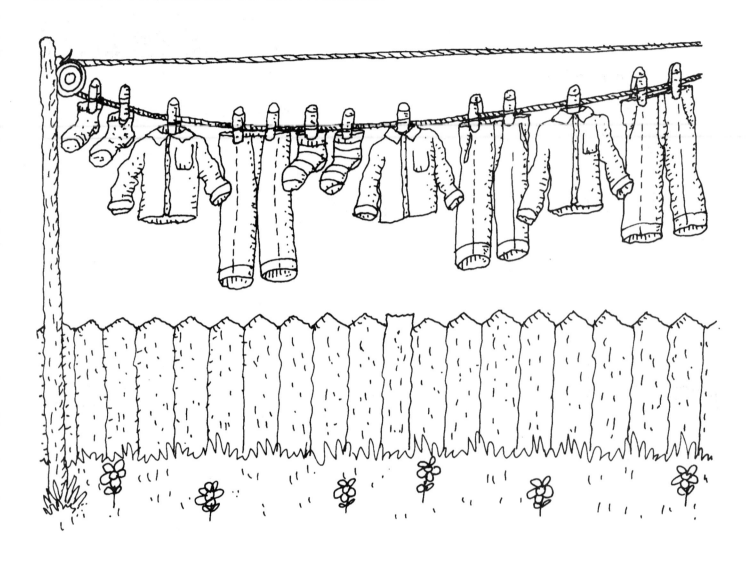

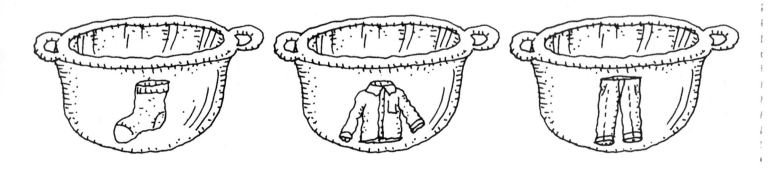

Skills: Classifying; Thinking logically

READING READINESS

Which things are alive?
Look at the pictures on this page.
Circle all the living things.
Put a line under all the things that are not alive.

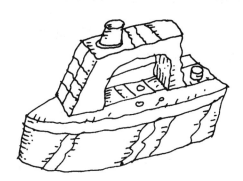

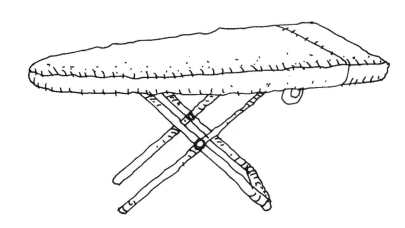

Skills: Classifying; Thinking logically

READING READINESS

Put the lowercase letters in the top box.
Put the uppercase letters in the bottom box.
Draw lines to connect each letter to its right box.

Skills: Classifying; Thinking logically; Recognizing upper and lowercase letters

READING READINESS

Let's collect shells!
Look at the shells and the piles below.
Draw lines to sort them into the correct piles.

Skills: Classifying; Thinking logically; Sorting

READING READINESS

Color all the circles red.
Color all the rectangles yellow.
Color all the triangles orange.
Color all the squares green.

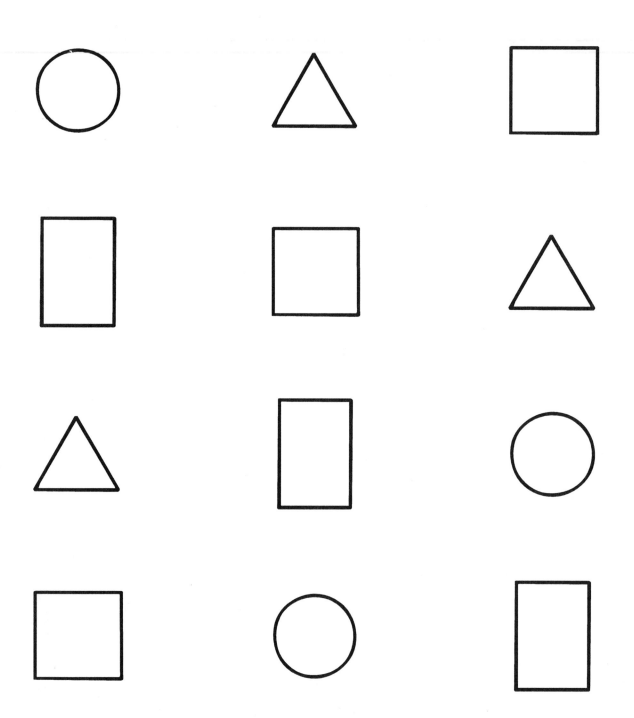

Skills: Classifying; Thinking logically; Sorting

READING READINESS

The bird wants to get to her nest.
Which path will get her there?

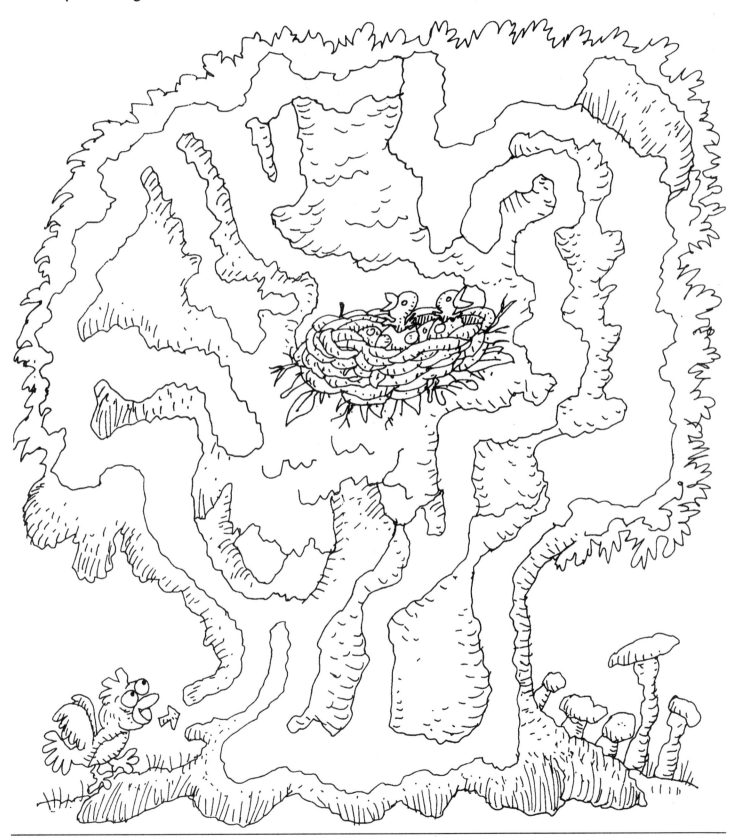

Skills: Visual perception; Developing fine motor skills; Thinking logically

READING READINESS

The train needs to get down the mountain.
Follow the path that leads to the station.

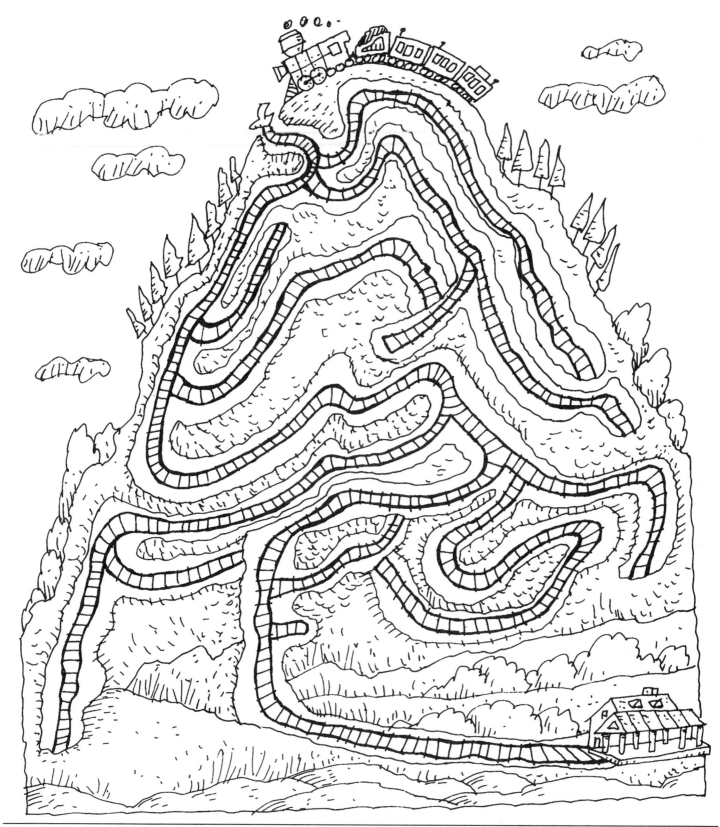

Skills: Visual perception; Developing fine motor skills

READING READINESS

Here comes the balloon!
Follow the path through the clouds to the landing site.

Skills: Visual perception; Developing fine motor skills

READING READINESS

Trace the lines to see who is flying each kite.

Skills: Visual perception; Developing fine motor skills

READING READINESS

The squirrels are looking for nuts.
Each squirrel will find a nut.
Follow each path to see what each squirrel finds.

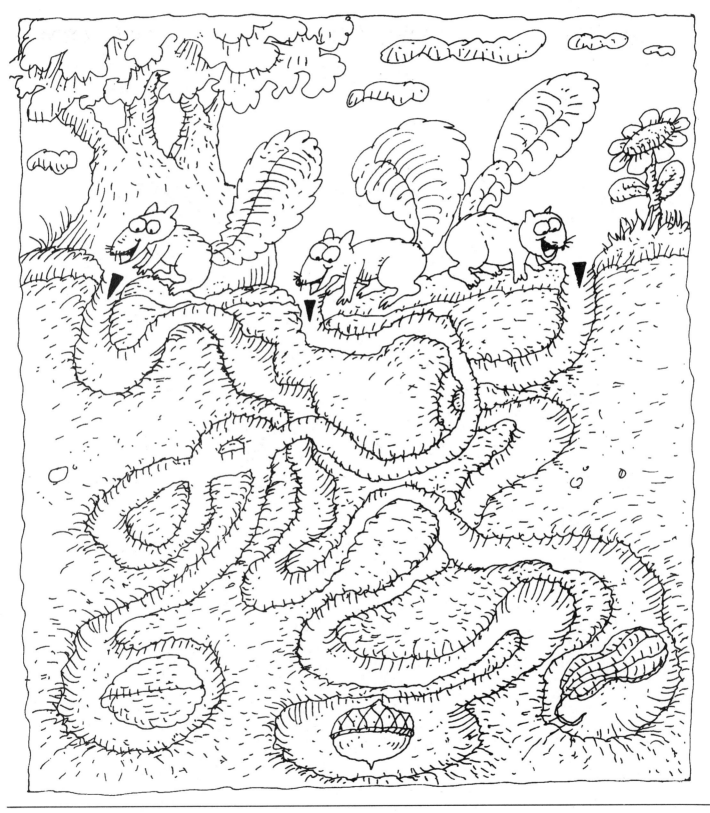

Skills: Visual perception; Developing fine motor skills

READING READINESS

It's time for the animals to sleep.
Follow the path from each animal.
Trace the lines to show where each animal goes to sleep.

Skills: Visual perception; Thinking logically; Developing fine motor skills; Eye/hand coordination

READING READINESS

What a cute doll!
Finish the picture of the doll so that both sides will
match exactly if it is folded on the dashed line.

Skills: Developing fine motor skills; Eye/hand coordination; Thinking logically

READING READINESS

Finish the picture of the butterfly so that both sides will match exactly if it is folded on the dashed line.

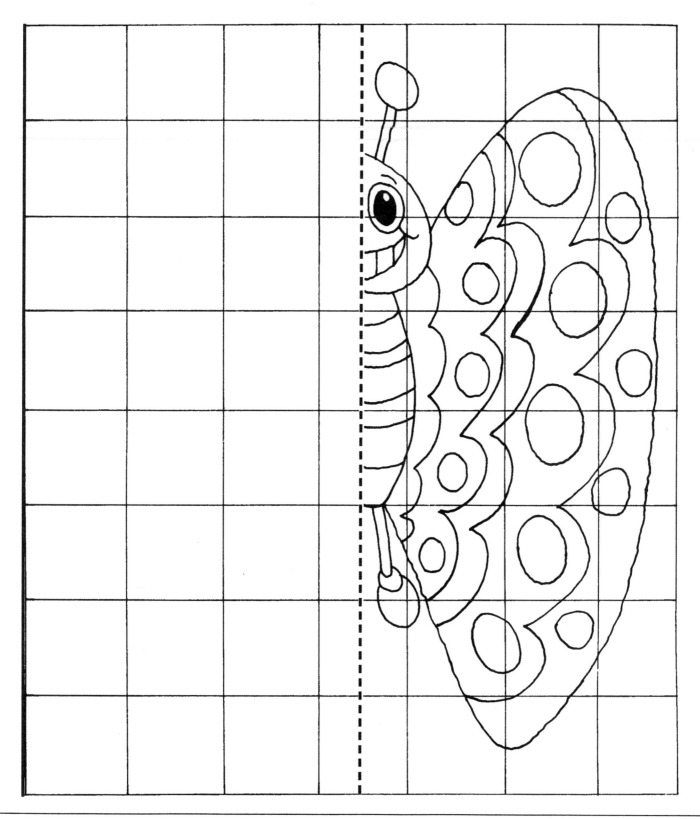

Skills: Developing fine motor skills; Eye/hand coordination; Thinking logically

READING READINESS

What is it?
Look at the unfinished picture.
Think about what it might be.
Complete the picture to show what you think it is.

Skills: Thinking logically; Developing fine motor skills; problem solving

READING READINESS

What will happen **next**?
Look at the scene on the left in each row.
Look at the two pictures on the right.
Circle the picture that shows what will happen next.
Then tell a story about the picture.

Skills: Sequencing; Predicting; Thinking logically

READING READINESS

What will happen **before**?
Look at the picture on the left in each row.
Look at the two pictures on the right.
Circle the picture that shows what will happen before.

Skills: Sequencing; Predicting; Thinking logically

READING READINESS

What happens next?
Look at the pictures at the top of the page.
Tell a story about the pictures.
Then draw a picture to show what happens next.

Skills: Sequencing; Thinking logically; Developing fine motor skills; Understanding story order

READING READINESS

What happens first? next? last?
The pictures in each row tell a story.
But they are mixed up.
Write the numbers 1, 2, 3 in the boxes to put the story in order.
Then tell the story.

Skills: Sequencing; Thinking logically; Understanding story order

READING READINESS

These pictures tell a story.
But the pictures are mixed up.
Write the numbers 1, 2, 3 and 4 in the boxes to put the story in order.
Then tell the story.

Skills: Sequencing; Thinking logically; Understanding story order

READING READINESS

Think about your day.
Look at the pictures on this page.
Circle the pictures that show things you use in the winter.
Underline the pictures that show things you use in summer.

Skills: Thinking logically

READING READINESS

Listen to the questions.
Circle your answers.

Which goes fastest?

Which is slowest?

Which is the smallest?

Which is the tallest?

Skills: Thinking logically; Problem solving

READING READINESS

Yummy!
Draw lines to connect each food on the right to
something that is made with it on the left.

Skills: Associating; Problem solving; Thinking logically

READING READINESS

Who is the real princess?
The real princess has bows in her hair and a rose on her dress.
Circle the real princess.

Skills: Deductive reasoning; Problem solving; Logical reasoning; Visual discrimination

READING READINESS

Who is in the playground?
Read the clues.
Then draw lines to connect each name to the correct child.

Katie is on the monkey bars.
David is on the swings.
Sandy and Mike are on the see-saw.
Where is Sam?

Skills: Thinking logically; Problem solving; Drawing conclusions

READING READINESS

Read the clues.
Then draw lines to connect each bunny name to the correct bunny.

Sunny is eating a carrot.
Honey is smelling a flower.
Benny is rolling in the grass.
Where is Penny?

Skills: Thinking logically; Problem solving; Drawing conclusions

PHONICS SKILLS I

Look at the pictures and the letters that make their ending sounds.
Look at the pictures and the letters at the bottom of the page.
Draw a line from each picture to the letter that makes its ending sound.

g   p   t

t

p

g

PHONICS SKILLS I

Look at the pictures and the letters that make their ending sounds.
Then look at the pictures and letters at the bottom of the page.
Draw a line from each picture to the letter that makes its ending sound.

t   k   s

Skills: Developing auditory discrimination; Matching ending sounds; Recognizing letter/sound relationships

PHONICS SKILLS I

Look at the letters on each easel.
Look at the picture on each easel.
Circle the picture whose name begins
with the sound that the letter makes.

Skills: Developing auditory discrimination; Matching beginning sounds; Recognizing
letter/sound relationships

PHONICS SKILLS I

Play this letter game.
Take turns tossing a penny or counter onto the house.
Name the letter that the penny falls on and a word that begins with that letter.
Collect 1 point for every correct answer.
The first person to reach 10 points wins.

Skills: Recognizing letter/sound relationships; Developing words for sounds

PHONICS SKILLS I

Look at the pictures and the letters that make their ending sounds.
Look at the pictures at the bottom of the page.
Draw a line between pictures with the same ending sound.

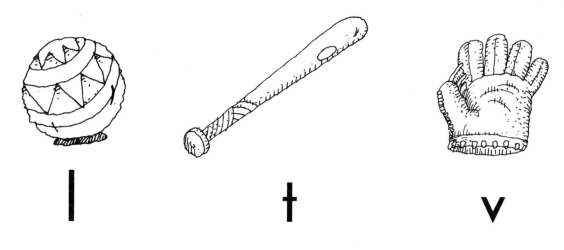

l   t   v

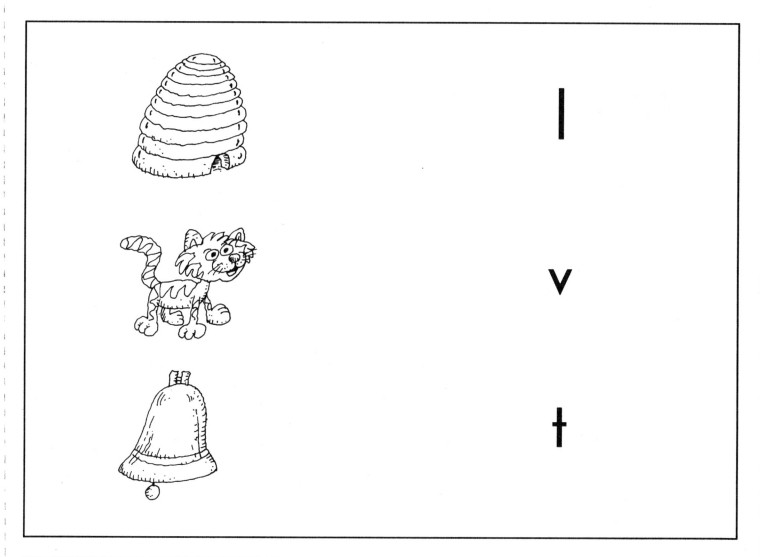

l

v

t

Skills: Developing auditory discrimination; Matching ending sounds; Recognizing letter/sound relationships

PHONICS SKILLS I

The balloon is trying to land.
Follow the vowels, **a**, **e**, **i**, **o**, **u**,
through the maze to the field.

Skills: Recognizing letters as vowels; Using visual perception skills; Developing fine motor skills

PHONICS SKILLS I

The family is going camping.
Follow the path of vowels, **A, E, I, O, U,**
through the maze to help them get to the campsite.

Skills: Recognizing letters as vowels; Using visual perception skills; Developing fine motor
skills

PHONICS SKILLS I

Look at the pictures on this set of blocks.
Sock has a short **o** sound. **Coat** has a long **o** sound.
Circle the pictures whose names have the short **o** sound.
Underline the pictures whose names have the long **o** sound.

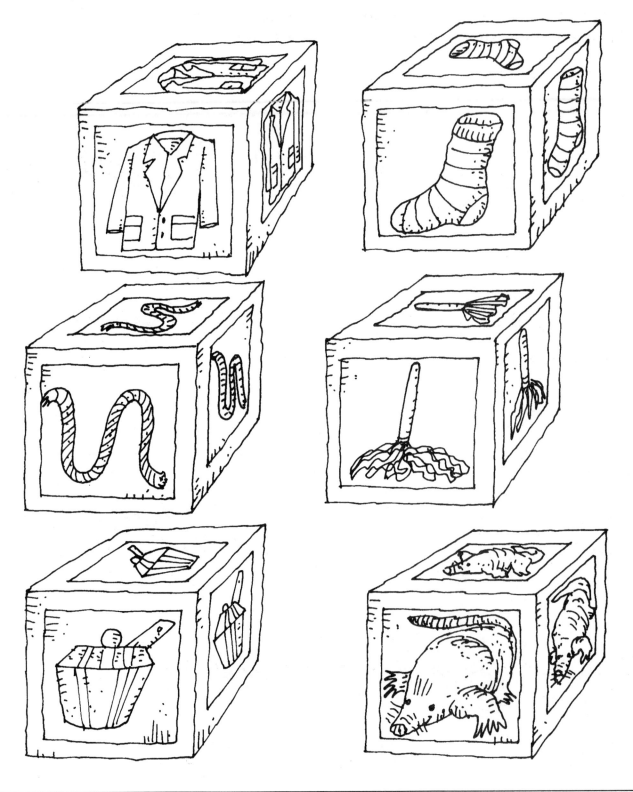

Skills: Using auditory discrimination skills; Understanding sound/symbol association;
Differentiating short and long vowel sounds

PHONICS SKILLS I

Let's have a party.

Put on a **hat**. Have some **cake**.

Hat has a short **a** sound. **Cake** has a long **a** sound.

Look at the pictures on this page.

Circle the pictures whose names have the short **a** sound.

Underline the pictures whose names have the long **a** sound.

Skills: Using auditory discrimination skills; Understanding sound/symbol association; Differentiating short and long vowel sounds

PHONICS SKILLS I

Initial Consonant: b

Print the letters and words.

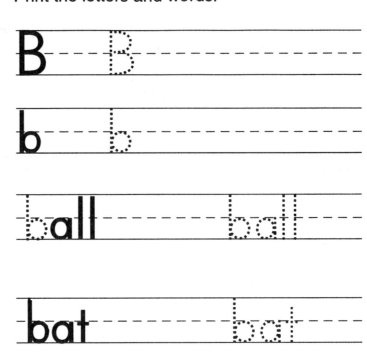

Finish the picture. Finish the word.

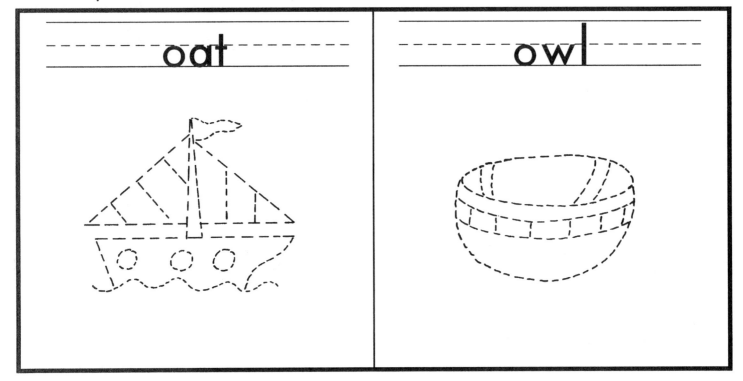

oat

owl

Skills: Recognition of the initial consonant "b"; Writing letters and words; Association between sounds, symbols, and words

246

PHONICS SKILLS I

Initial Consonant: f

Print the letters and words.

F   F

f   f

fairy   fairy

fish   fish

Finish the picture. Finish the word.

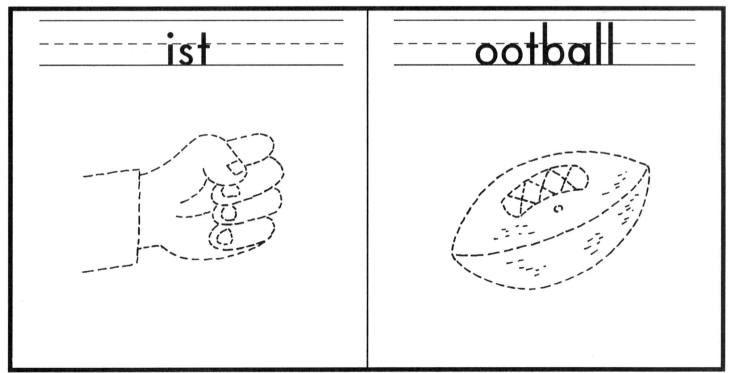

ist   ootball

Skills: Recognition of the initial consonant "f"; Writing letters and words; Association between sounds, symbols, and words

PHONICS SKILLS I

Initial Consonant: **g**

Print the letters and words.

G   G

g   g

gorilla   gorilla

gull   gull

Finish the picture. Finish the word.

old

oose

Skills: Recognition of the initial consonant "g"; Writing letters and words; Association between sounds, symbols, and words

PHONICS SKILLS I

Initial Consonant: k

Print the letters and words.

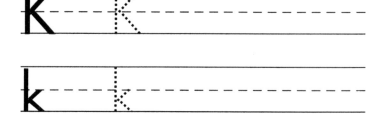

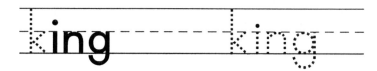

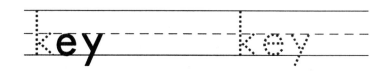

Finish the picture. Finish the word.

iwi

angaroo

Skills: Recognition of the initial consonant "k"; Writing letters and words; Association between sounds, symbols, and words

PHONICS SKILLS I

Initial Consonant: v

Print the letters and words.

V ---- v --------------------

v ---- v --------------------

veil ---- veil ----

vest ---- vest ----

Finish the picture. Finish the word.

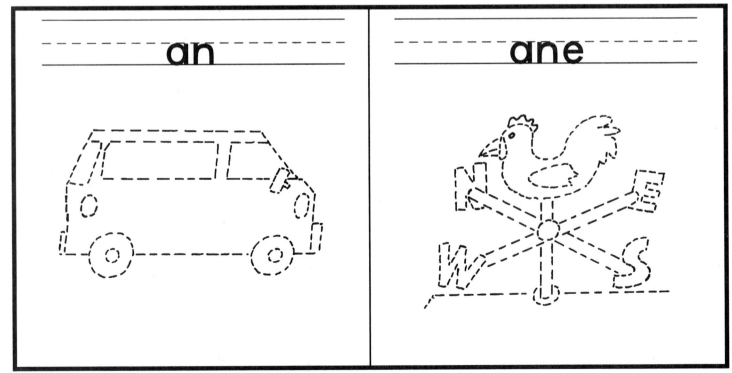

an

ane

Skills: Recognition of the initial consonant "v"; Writing letters and words; Association between sounds, symbols, and words

PHONICS SKILLS I

Initial Consonant: c

Print the letters and words.

C C

c c

cone   cone

cow   cow

Finish the picture. Finish the word.

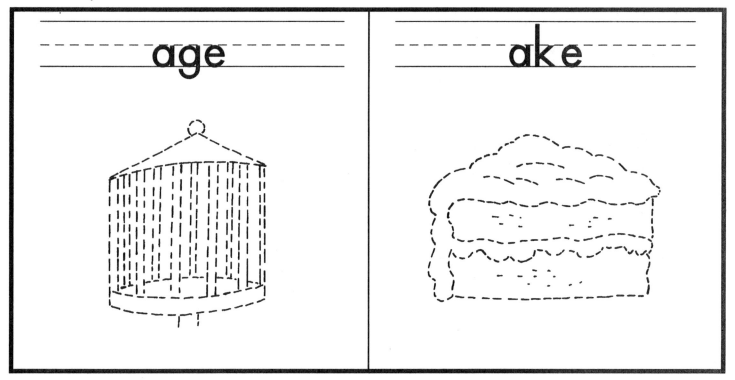

age

ake

Skills: Recognition of the initial consonant "c"; Writing letters and words; Association between sounds, symbols, and words

PHONICS SKILLS I

Initial Consonant: h

Print the letters and words.

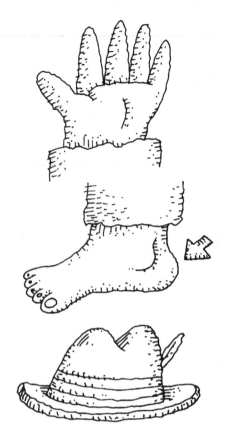

hat ------ hat

Finish the picture. Finish the word.

og

ouse

Skills: Recognition of the initial consonant "h"; Writing letters and words; Association between sounds, symbols and words

252

PHONICS SKILLS I

Initial Consonant: **m**

Print the letters and words.

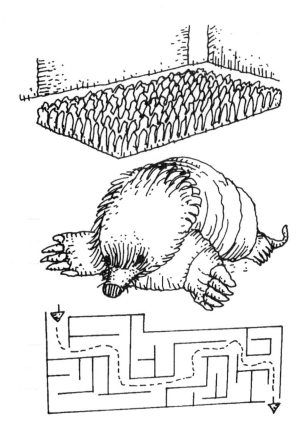

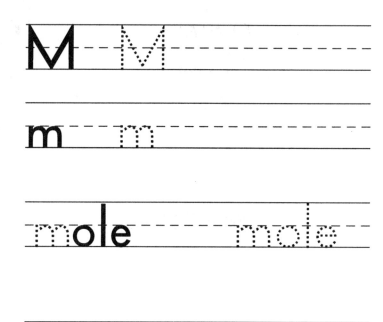

Finish the picture. Finish the word.

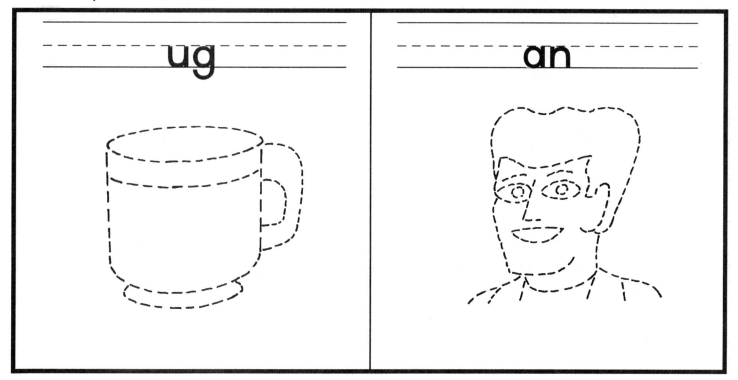

Skills: Recognition of the initial consonant "m"; Writing letters and words; Association between sounds, symbols, and words

PHONICS SKILLS I

Initial Consonant: p

Print the letters and words.

P ⎯ P ⎯ ⎯ ⎯ ⎯ ⎯ ⎯ ⎯ ⎯ ⎯

p ⎯ p ⎯ ⎯ ⎯ ⎯ ⎯ ⎯ ⎯ ⎯ ⎯

pot   pot

pail   pail

Finish the picture. Finish the word.

ig

aint

Skills: Recognition of the initial consonant "p"; Writing letters and words; Association between sounds, symbols, and words

PHONICS SKILLS I

Initial Consonant: y

Print the letters and words.

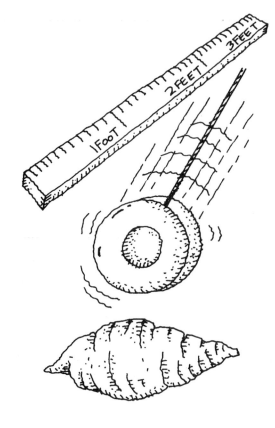

Y Y

y y

yo-yo   yo-yo

yam   yam

Finish the picture. Finish the word.

arn

ak

Skills: Recognition of the initial consonant "y"; Writing letters and words; Association between sounds, symbols, and words

PHONICS SKILLS I

Initial Consonant: d

Print the letters and words.

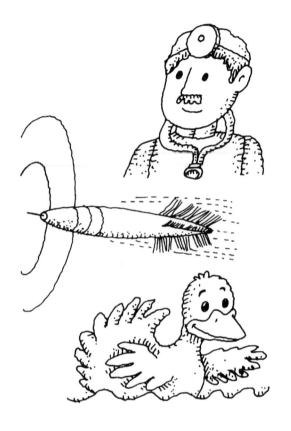

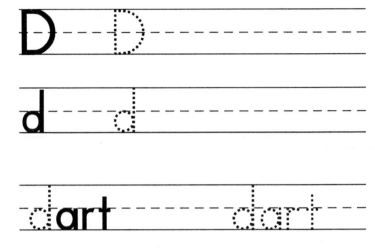

D   D

d   d

dart   dart

duck   duck

Finish the picture. Finish the word.

aisy

og

Skills: Recognition of the initial consonant "d"; Writing letters and words; Association between sounds, symbols, and words

256

PHONICS SKILLS I

Initial Consonant: j

Print the letters and words.

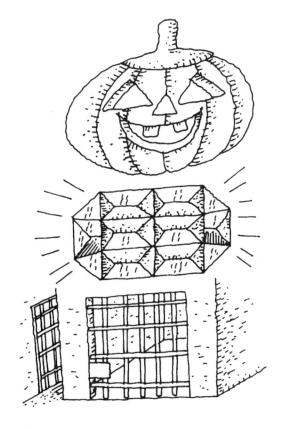

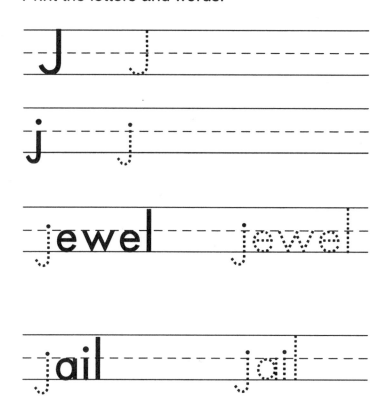

J   J

j   j

jewel   jewel

jail   jail

Finish the picture. Finish the word.

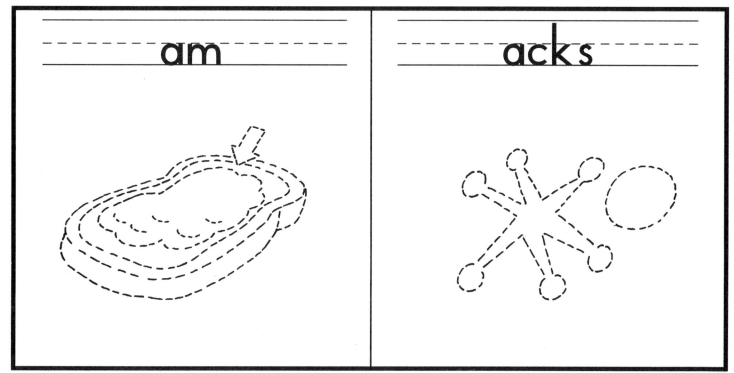

___am

___acks

Skills: Recognition of the initial consonant "j"; Writing letters and words; Association between sounds, symbols, and words

PHONICS SKILLS I

Initial Consonant: l

Print the letters and words.

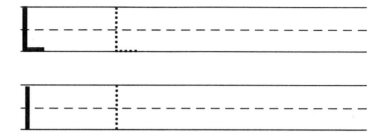

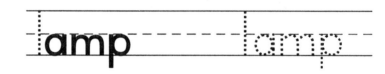

Finish the picture. Finish the word.

Skills: Recognition of the initial consonant "l"; Writing letters and words; Association between sounds, symbols, and words

258

PHONICS SKILLS I

Initial Consonant: **w**

Print the letters and words.

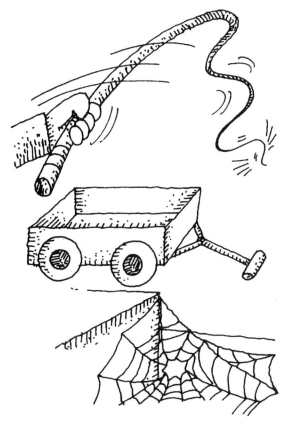

W   W

w   w

wagon   wagon

web   web

Finish the picture. Finish the word.

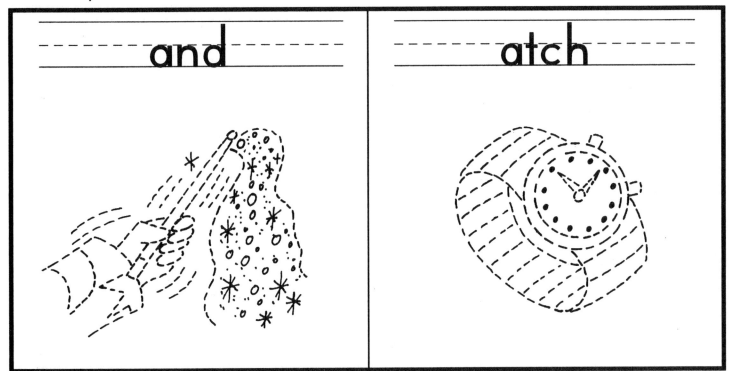

and

atch

Skills: Recognition of the initial consonant "w"; Writing letters and words; Association between sounds, symbols, and words

PHONICS SKILLS I

Initial Consonant: **z**

Print the letters and words.

Z   Z

z   z

zebra   zebra

zoom   zoom

Finish the picture. Finish the word.

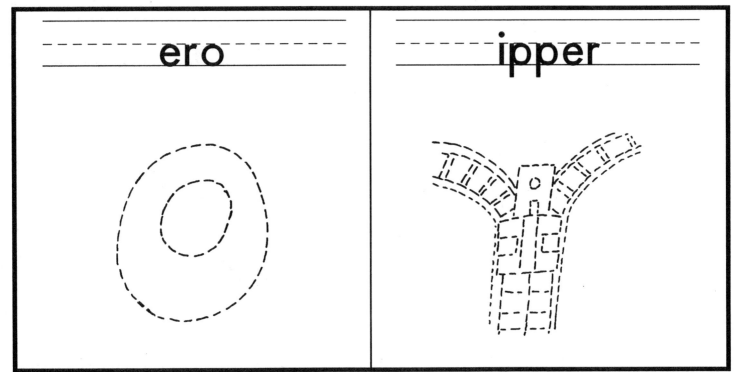

ero

ipper

Skills: Recognition of the initial consonant "z"; Writing letters and words; Association between sounds, symbols, and words

PHONICS SKILLS I

Initial Consonant: n

Print the letters and words.

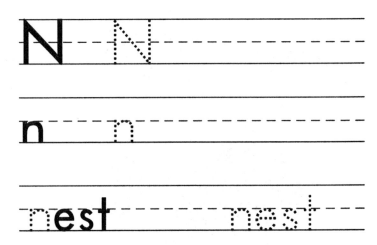

N N

n n

nest   nest

note   note

Finish the picture. Finish the word.

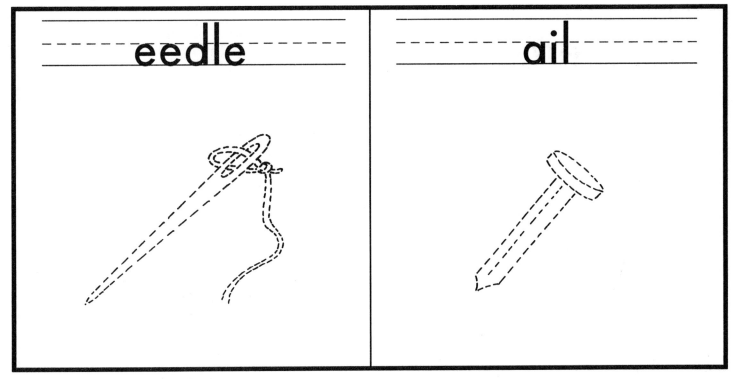

eedle

ail

Skills: Recognition of the initial consonant "n"; Writing letters and words; Association between sounds, symbols, and words

PHONICS SKILLS I

Initial Consonant: q

Print the letters and words.

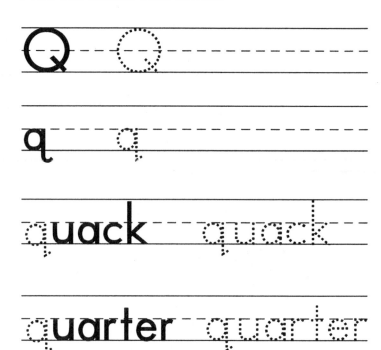

Finish the picture. Finish the word.

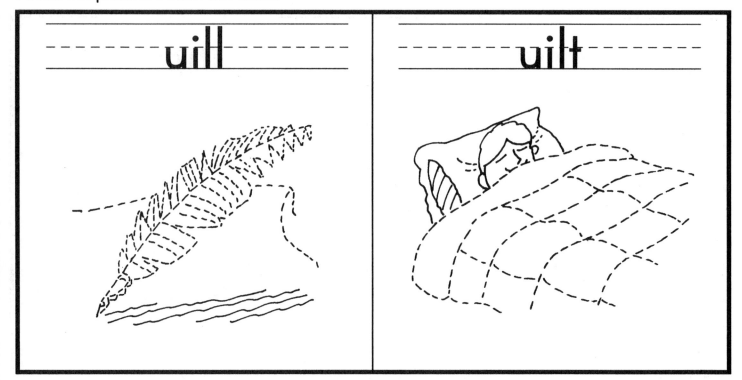

Skills: Recognition of the initial consonant "q"; Writing letters and words; Association between sounds, symbols, and words

PHONICS SKILLS I

Initial Consonant: r

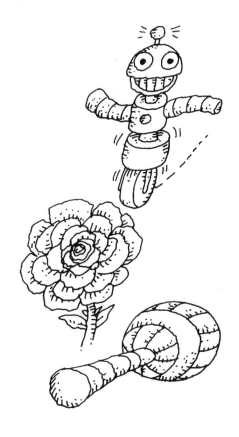

Print the letters and words.

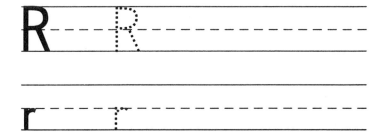

R   R

r   r

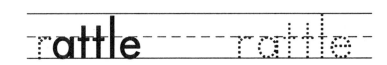

rose   rose

rattle   rattle

Finish the picture. Finish the word.

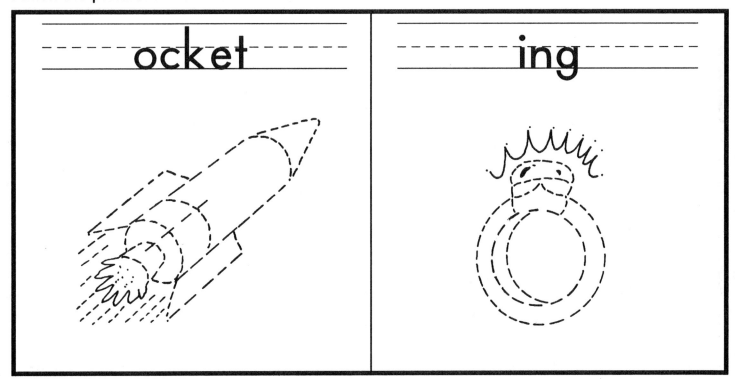

ocket

ing

Skills: Recognition of the initial consonant "r"; Writing letters and words; Association between sounds, symbols, and words

PHONICS SKILLS I

Initial Consonant: **s**

Print the letters and words.

S S

s s

sack   sack

santa   santa

Finish the picture. Finish the word.

aw

ailor

Skills: Recognition of the initial consonant "s"; Writing letters and words; Association between sounds, symbols, and words

PHONICS SKILLS I

Initial Consonant: t

Print the letters and words.

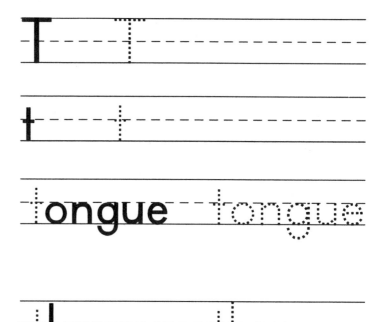

T T

t t

tongue   tongue

three   three

Finish the picture. Finish the word.

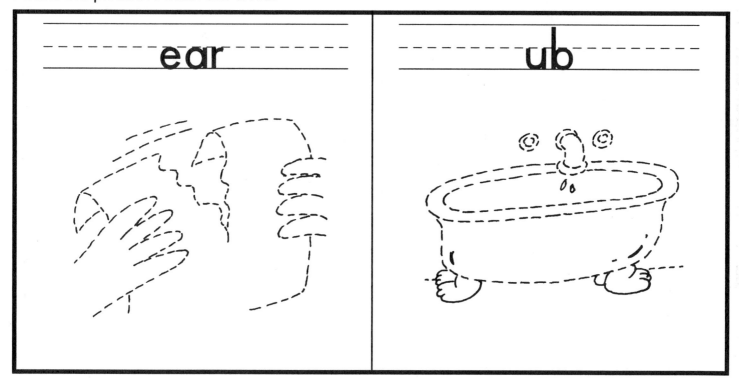

ear

ub

Skills: Recognition of the initial consonant "t"; Writing letters and words; Association between sounds, symbols, and words

PHONICS SKILLS I

Final consonant: b

cra b

b b

Which ones end with **b**? Color them orange. Color the other pictures blue.

Skills: Recognition of the final consonant "b"; Auditory discrimination; Writing the letter "b"; Sound/symbol association

Final consonant: f

thief

f

Which ones end with **f**? Color them red. Color the other pictures green.

Skills: Recognition of the final consonant "f"; Auditory discrimination; Writing the letter "f"; Sound/symbol association

PHONICS SKILLS I

Final consonant: d

s l e d

d

Which ones end with **d**? Color them yellow. Color the other pictures red.

Skills: Recognition of the final consonant "d"; Auditory discrimination; Writing the letter "d"; Sound/symbol association

PHONICS SKILLS I

Final consonant: **g**

do**g**

g

Which ones end with **g**? Color them brown. Color the other pictures blue.

Skills: Recognition of the final consonant "g"; Auditory discrimination; Writing the letter "g"; Sound/symbol association

PHONICS SKILLS I

Final consonant: k

SOC k

k k

Which ones end with **k**? Color them blue. Color the other pictures red.

Skills: Recognition of the final consonant "k"; Auditory discrimination; Writing the letter "k"; Sound/symbol association

PHONICS SKILLS I

Final consonant: **m**

dru**m**

m **m**

Which ones end with **m**? Color them orange. Color the other pictures red.

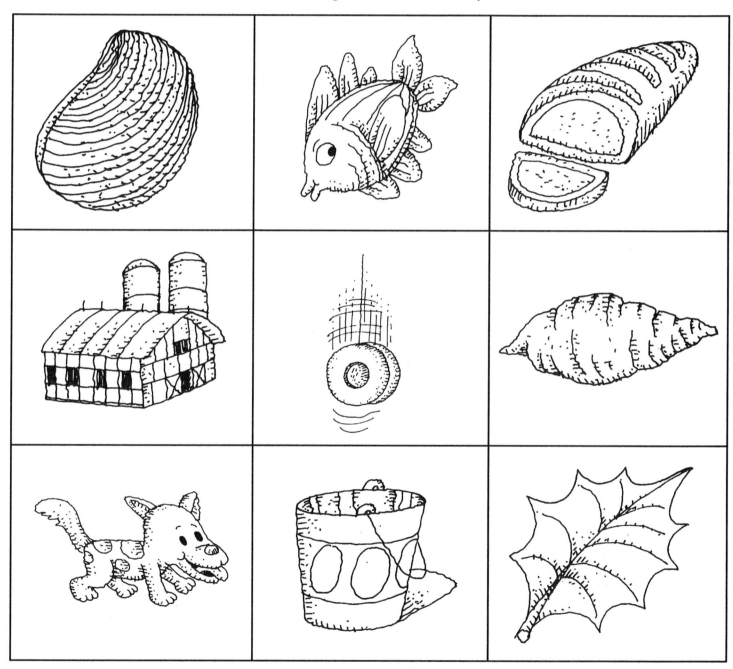

Skills: Recognition of the final consonant "m"; Auditory discrimination; Writing the letter "m"; Sound/symbol association

PHONICS SKILLS I

Final consonant: l

pai

l

Which ones end with l? Color them red. Color the other pictures blue.

Skills: Recognition of the final consonant "l"; Auditory discrimination; Writing the letter "l"; Sound/symbol association

272

PHONICS SKILLS I

Final consonant: **n**

ma n

n n

Which ones end with **n**? Color them green. Color the other pictures yellow.

Skills: Recognition of the final consonant "n"; Auditory discrimination; Writing the letter "n"; Sound/symbol association

PHONICS SKILLS I

Final consonant: **p**

jeep

p p

Which ones end with **p**? Color them red. Color the other pictures green.

Skills: Recognition of the final consonant "p"; Auditory discrimination; Writing the letter "p"; Sound/symbol association

PHONICS SKILLS I

Final consonant: **r**

bea

r

Which ones end with **r**? Color them brown. Color the other pictures green.

Skills: Recognition of the final consonant "r"; Auditory discrimination; Writing the letter "r"; Sound/symbol association

PHONICS SKILLS I

Final consonant: t

boat

t

Which ones end with **t**? Color them yellow. Color the other pictures blue.

Skills: Recognition of the final consonant "t"; Auditory discrimination; Writing the letter "t"; Sound/symbol association

PHONICS SKILLS I

Final consonant: **x**

fox

x x

Which ones end with **x**? Color them green. Color the other pictures brown.

Skills: Recognition of the final consonant "x"; Auditory discrimination; Writing the letter "x";
Sound/symbol association

PHONICS SKILLS II

Short vowel: ă

Print the letters and words.

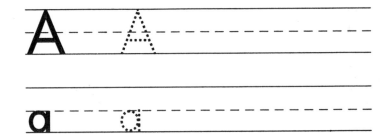

A   A

a   a

bat   bat

can   can

Finish the picture. Finish the word.

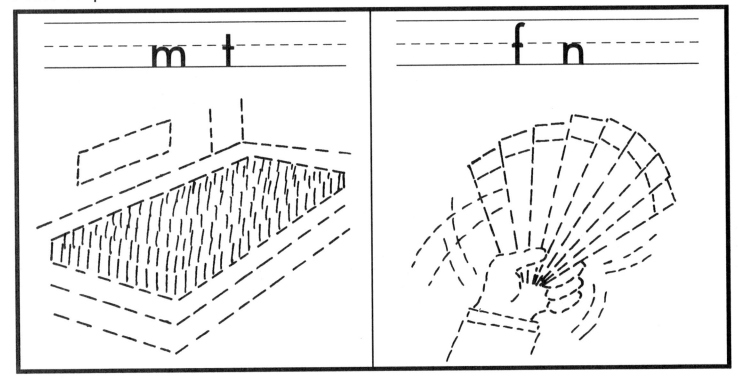

m t

f n

Skills: Recognition of the short vowel "a"; Writing letters and words; Association between sounds, symbols, and words

PHONICS SKILLS II

Short vowel: ă

A   A

a   a

Which ones have the ă sound? Color them blue. Color the other pictures green.

Skills: Recognition of the short vowel "a"; Auditory discrimination; Writing the letter "a"; Sound/symbol association

PHONICS SKILLS II

Short vowel: ĕ

Print the letters and words.

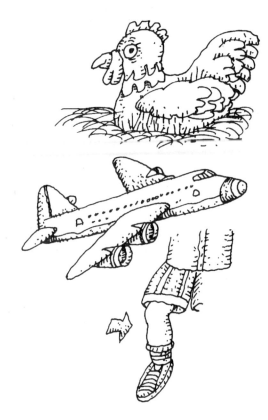

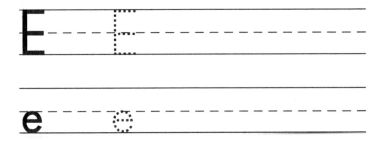

E   E

e   e

j e t   j e t

l e g   l e g

Finish the picture. Finish the word.

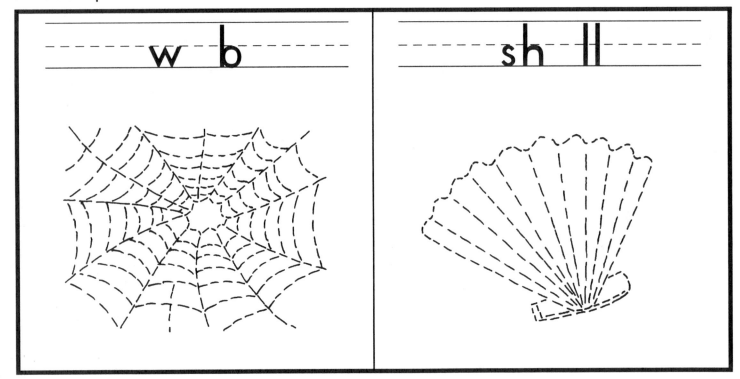

w   b   sh   ll

Skills: Recognition of the short vowel "e"; Writing letters and words; Association between sounds, symbols, and words

PHONICS SKILLS II

Short vowel: ĕ

E

e

Which ones have the ĕ sound? Color them blue. Color the other pictures yellow.

Skills: Recognition of the short vowel "e"; Auditory discrimination; Writing the letter "e"; Sound/symbol association

PHONICS SKILLS II

Short vowel: ĭ

Print the letters and words.

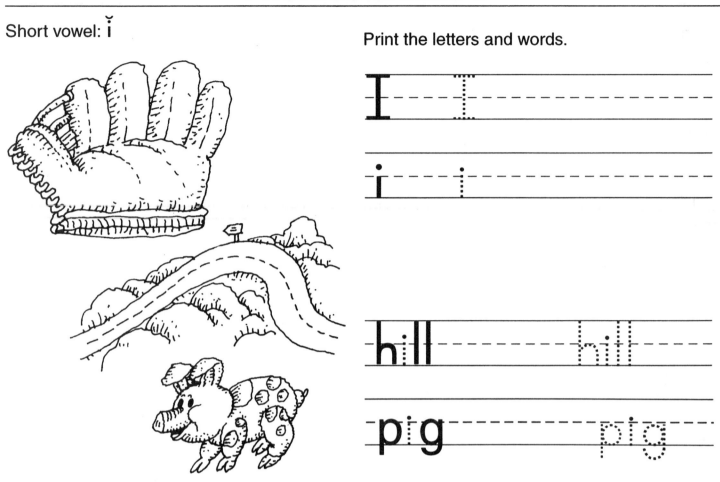

I   I

i   i

hill   hill

pig   pig

Finish the picture. Finish the word.

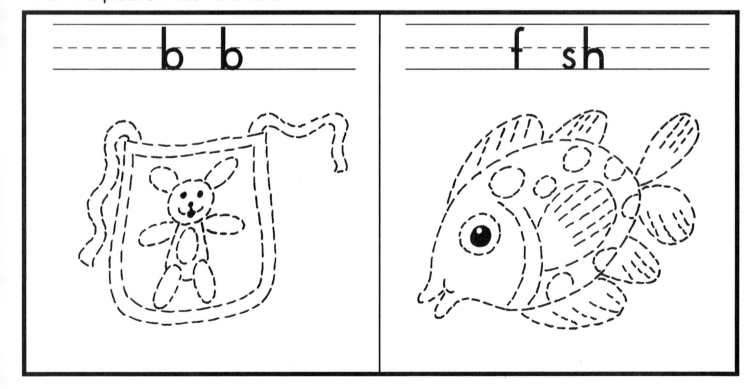

b   b

f   sh

Skills: Recognition of the short vowel "i"; Writing letters and words; Association between sounds, symbols, and words

PHONICS SKILLS II

Short vowel: ĭ

I - - - - - - - - - - - - - -

i - - - - - - - - - - - - - -

Which have the ĭ sound? Color them green. Color the other pictures brown.

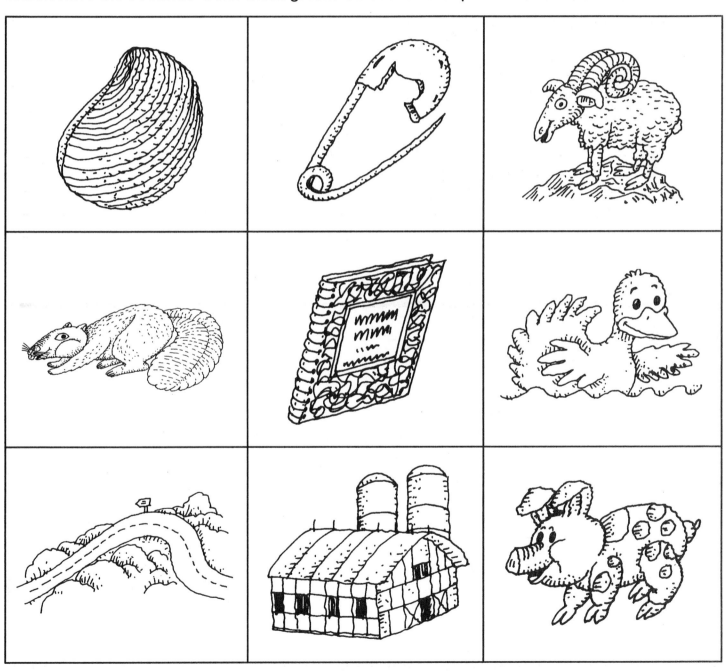

Skills: Recognition of the short vowel "i"; Auditory discrimination; Writing the letter "i"; Sound/symbol association

PHONICS SKILLS II

Short vowel: ŏ

Print the letters and words.

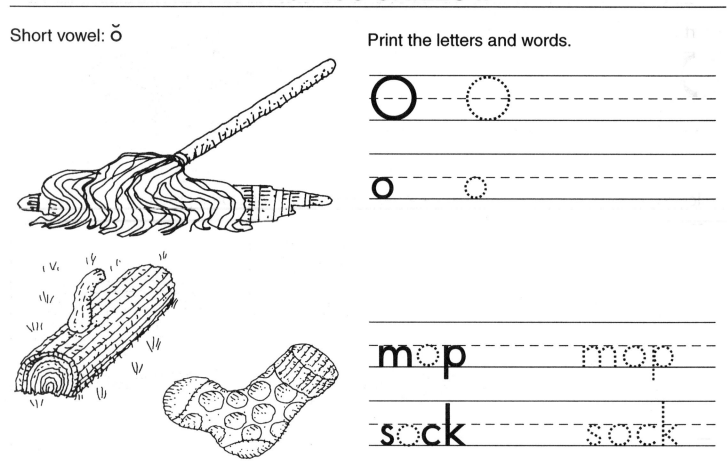

O ⭕

o ○

mop   mop

sock   sock

Finish the picture. Finish the word.

d ll

t t

Skills: Recognition of the short vowel "o"; Writing letters and words; Association between sounds, symbols, and words

PHONICS SKILLS II

Short vowel: ŏ

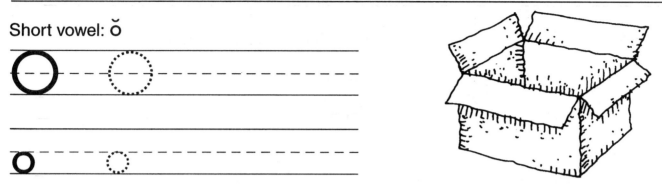

Which have the **ŏ** sound? Color them orange. Color the other pictures green.

Skills: Recognition of the short vowel "o"; Auditory discrimination; Writing the letter "o"; Sound/symbol association

PHONICS SKILLS II

Short vowel: ŭ

Print the letters and words.

U   U

u   u

drum   drum

bug   bug

Finish the picture. Finish the word.

t b

d ck

Skills: Recognition of the short vowel "u"; Writing letters and words; Association between sounds, symbols, and words

PHONICS SKILLS II

Short vowel: ŭ

U ‒‒‒‒‒‒‒‒‒‒‒‒‒‒‒‒‒‒‒‒‒‒‒‒‒‒

u ‒‒‒‒‒‒‒‒‒‒‒‒‒‒‒‒‒‒‒‒‒‒‒‒‒‒

Which have the ŭ sound? Color them red. Color the other pictures yellow.

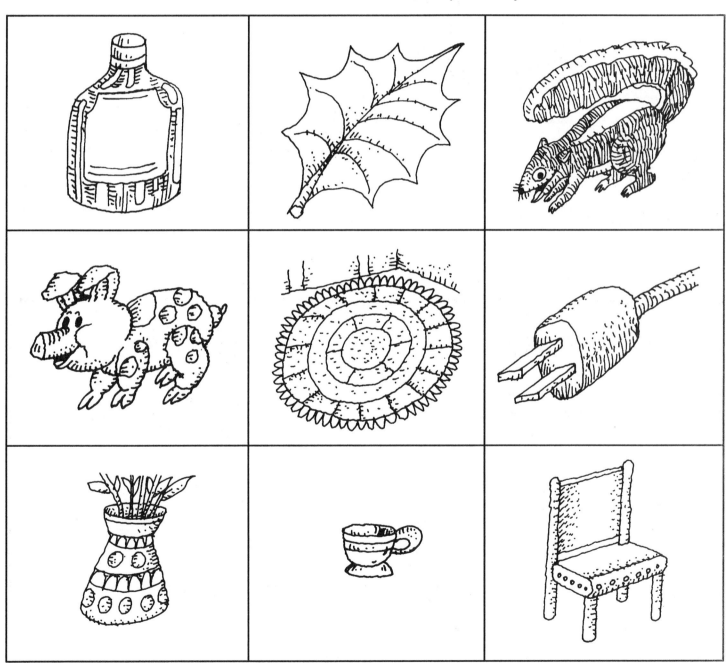

Skills: Recognition of the short vowel "u"; Auditory discrimination; Writing the letter "u"; Sound/symbol association

PHONICS SKILLS II

Short vowels: ă, ĕ, ĭ, ŏ, ŭ

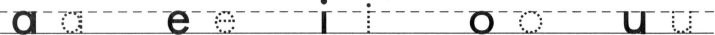

Say the name of each picture. Listen to the vowel sound. Then circle the vowel and print the letter.

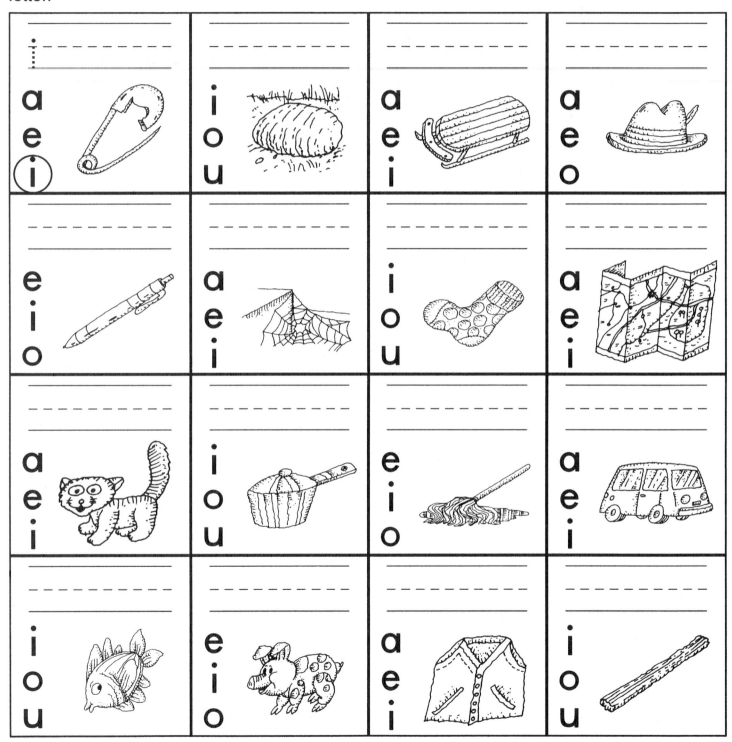

Skills: Recognition of the short vowel sounds; Writing letters; Auditory and visual discrimination

PHONICS SKILLS II

Long vowel: ā

Print the letters and words.

A A A

a a

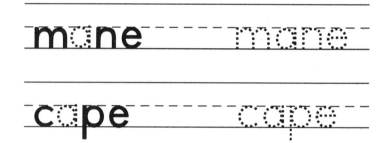

mane mane

cape cape

Finish the picture. Finish the word.

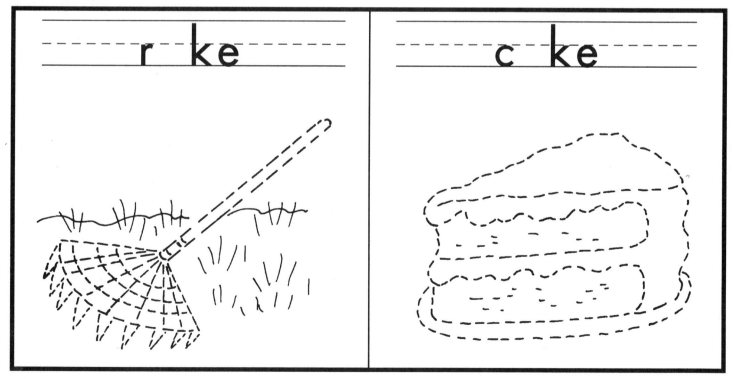

r ke

c ke

Skills: Recognition of the long vowel "a"; Writing letters and words; Association between sounds, symbols, and words

PHONICS SKILLS II

Long vowel: ā

A A

a a

Which ones have the ā sound? Color them red. Color the other pictures blue.

Skills: Recognition of the long vowel "a"; Auditory discrimination; Writing the letter "a"; Sound/symbol association

PHONICS SKILLS II

Long vowel: ē

Print the letters and words.

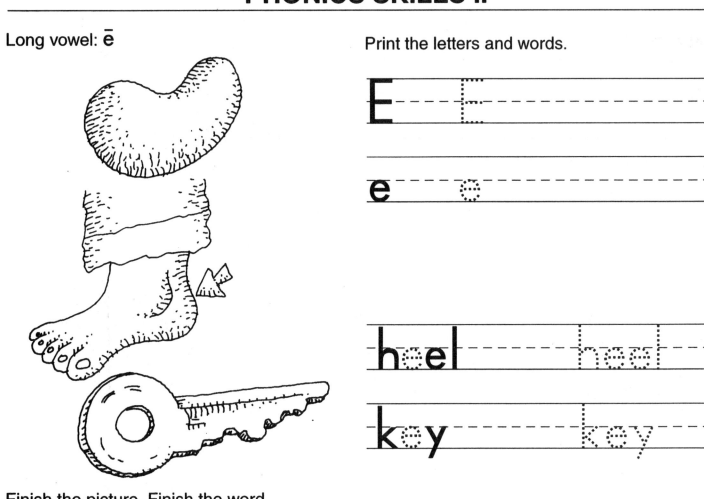

E   E

e   e

heel   heel

key   key

Finish the picture. Finish the word.

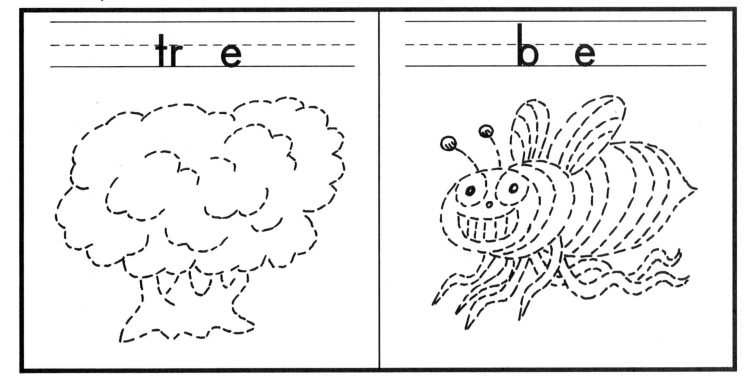

tr __ e

b __ e

Skills: Recognition of the long vowel "e"; Writing letters and words; Association between sounds, symbols, and words

PHONICS SKILLS II

Long vowel: ē

E

e

Which ones have the ē sound? Color them green. Color the other pictures blue.

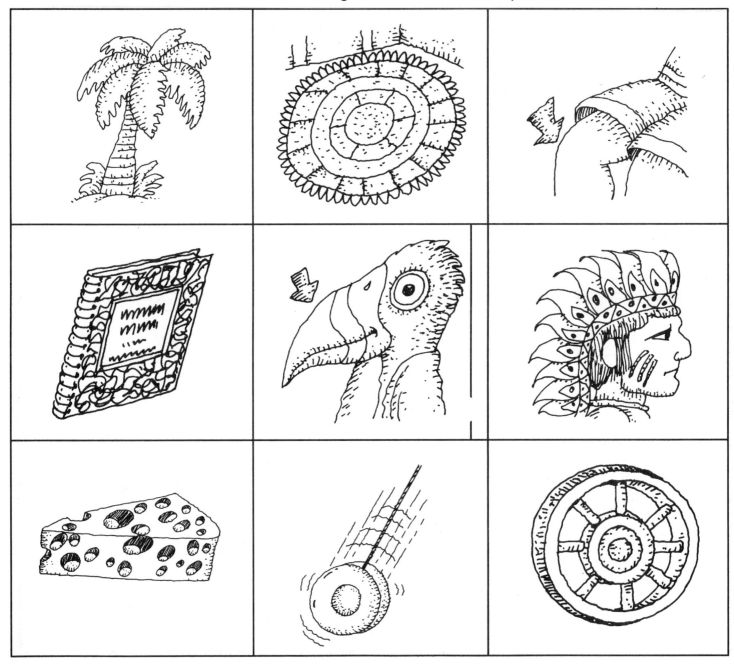

Skills: Recognition of the long vowel "e"; Auditory discrimination; Writing the letter "e"; Sound/symbol association

PHONICS SKILLS II

Long vowel: ī

Print the letters and words.

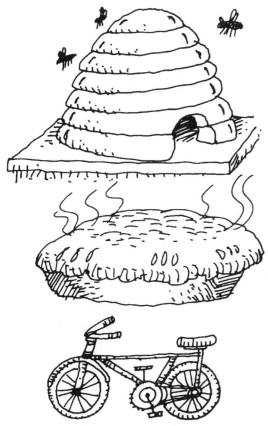

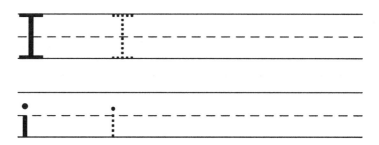

I   I

i   i

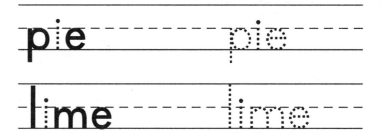

pie   pie

lime   lime

Finish the picture. Finish the word.

d me

k te

Skills: Recognition of the long vowel "i"; Writing letters and words; Association between sounds, symbols, and words

293

PHONICS SKILLS II

Long vowel: ī

I - - - - - - - - - - - - - - - -

i - - - - i - - - - - - - - - - -

Which ones have the ī sound? Color them yellow. Color the other pictures red.

Skills: Recognition of the long vowel "i"; Auditory discrimination; Writing the letter "i"; Sound/symbol association

PHONICS SKILLS II

Long vowel: ō

Print the letters and words.

O   O _____

o   o _____

hoe   hoe

note   note

Finish the picture. Finish the word.

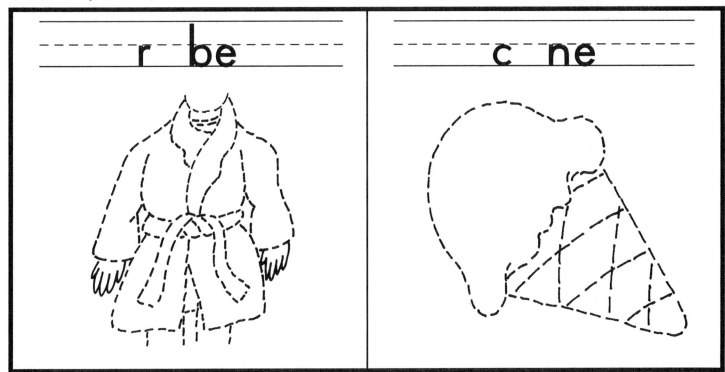

r be   c ne

Skills: Recognition of the long vowel "o"; Writing letters and words; Association between sounds, symbols, and words

295

PHONICS SKILLS II

Long vowel: ō

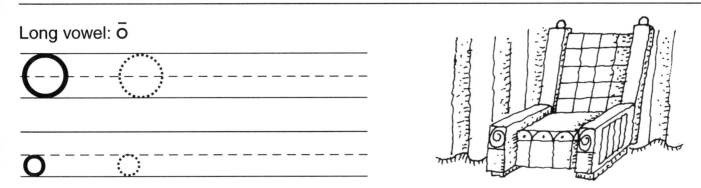

Which ones have the ō sound? Color them brown. Color the other pictures blue.

Skills: Recognition of the long vowel "o"; Auditory discrimination; Writing the letter "o"; Sound/symbol association

PHONICS SKILLS II

Long vowel: ū

Print the letters and words.

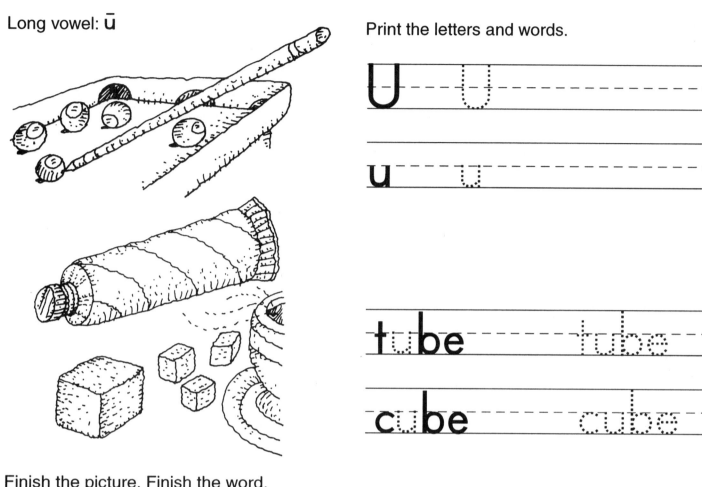

U U

u u

tube   tube

cube   cube

Finish the picture. Finish the word.

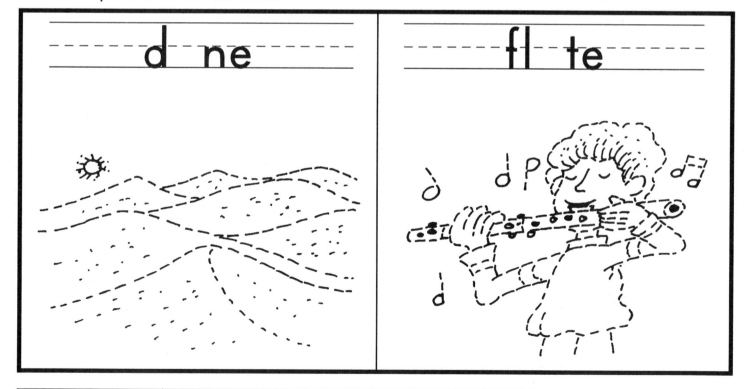

d ne

fl te

Skills: Recognition of the long vowel "u"; Writing letters and words; Association between sounds, symbols, and words

PHONICS SKILLS II

Long vowel: ū

U — U

u — u

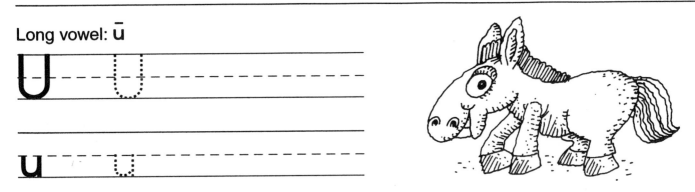

Which ones have the ū sound? Color them green. Color the other pictures red.

Skills: Recognition of the long vowel "u"; Auditory discrimination; Writing the letter "u"; Sound/symbol association

PHONICS SKILLS II

Long vowels: ā, ē, ī, ō, ū

a a e e i i o o u u

Say the name of each picture. Listen to the vowel sound. Then circle the vowel and print the letter.

Skills: Recognition of the long vowel sounds; Writing letters; Auditory and visual discrimination

PHONICS SKILLS II

Long and short vowel: a

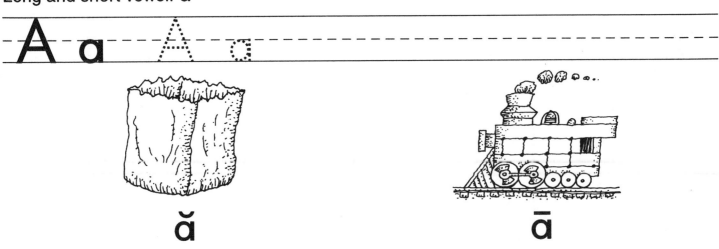

ă

ā

Which ones have the ă sound? Color them red.
Which ones have the ā sound? Color them blue.

Skills: Auditory and visual discrimination; Sound/Symbol association; Writing the letter "a"

PHONICS SKILLS II

Long and short vowel: e

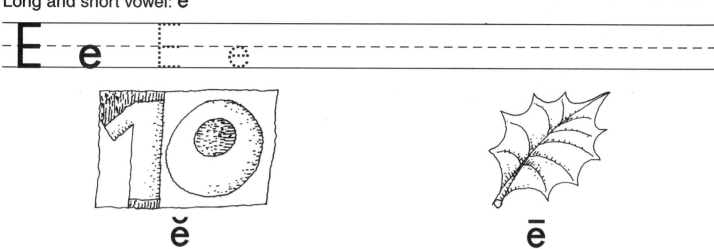

Which ones have the ĕ sound? Color them green.
Which ones have the ē sound? Color them yellow.

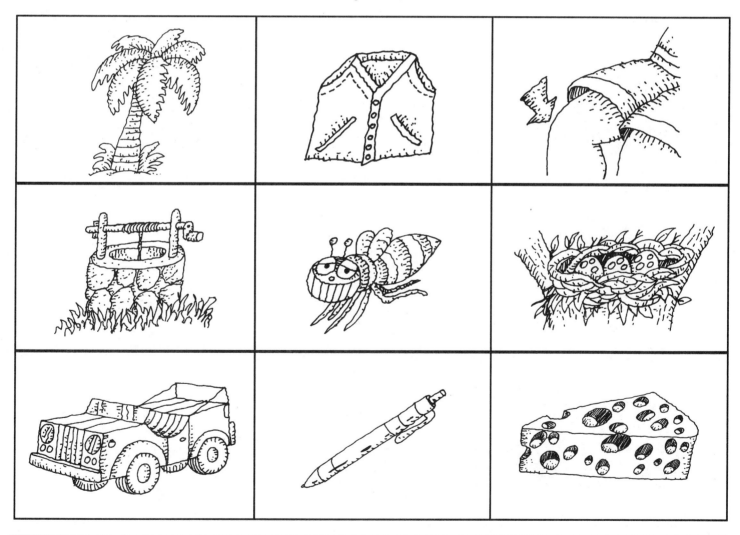

Skills: Auditory and visual discrimination; Sound/Symbol association; Writing the letter "e"

PHONICS SKILLS II

Long and short vowel: i

I i

Which ones have the ĭ sound? Color them orange.
Which ones have the ī sound? Color them yellow.

Skills: Auditory and visual discrimination; Sound/Symbol association; Writing the letter "i"

PHONICS SKILLS II

Long and short vowel: o

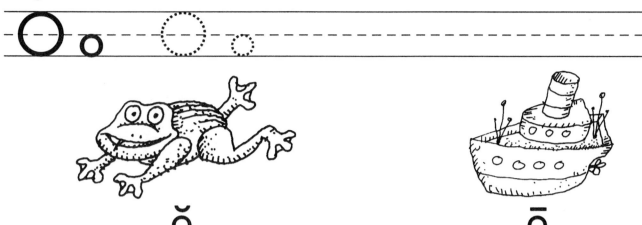

ŏ   ō

Which ones have the ŏ sound? Color them blue.
Which ones have the ō sound? Color them green.

Skills: Auditory and visual discrimination; Sound/Symbol association; Writing the letter "o"

PHONICS SKILLS II

Long and short vowel: **u**

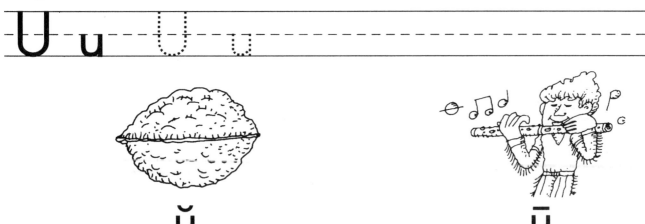

Which ones have the **ŭ** sound? Color them green.
Which ones have the **ū** sound? Color them red.

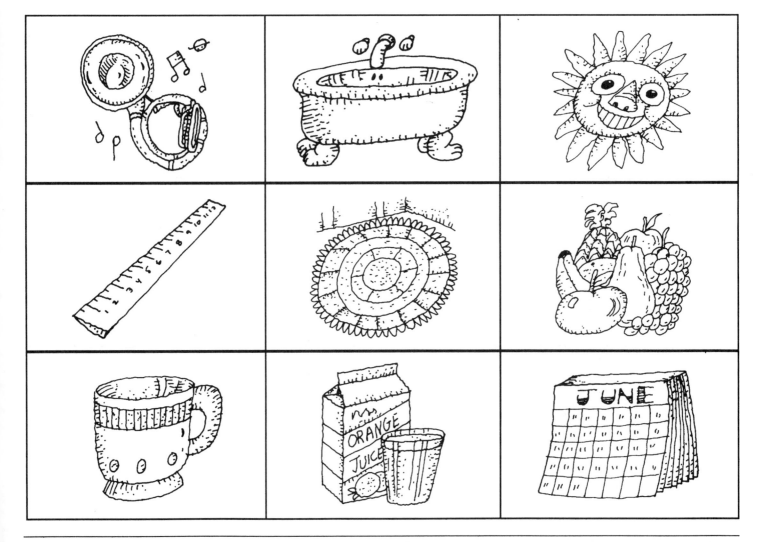

Skills: Auditory and visual discrimination; Sound/Symbol association; Writing the letter "u"

PHONICS SKILLS II

Long and short vowels: a , e , i , o , u

a a   e e   i i   o o   u u

Say the name of each picture. Listen to the vowel sound. Then print the vowel you hear.

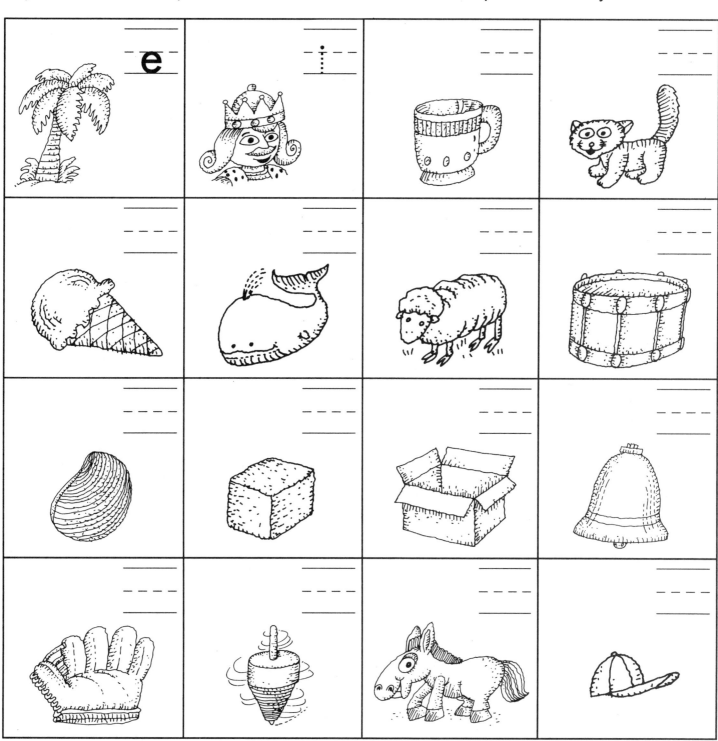

Skills: Recognition of the long and short vowel sounds; Writing letters; Auditory and visual discrimination

PHONICS SKILLS II

Initial consonant blends: cl, cr

cl

cr

Which ones begin with cl? Color them blue.
Which ones begin with cr? Color them green.

Skills: Understanding that some consonant sounds can be blended together; Sound/symbol association

PHONICS SKILLS II

Initial consonant blends: bl, br

bl

br

Which ones begin with bl? Color them black.
Which ones begin with br? Color them brown.

Skills: Understanding that some consonant sounds can be blended together; Sound/symbol association

PHONICS SKILLS II

Initial consonant blends: dr , tr

d r -

t r -

Which ones begin with dr? Color them blue.
Which ones begin with tr? Color them red.

Skills: Understanding that some consonant sounds can be blended together; Sound/symbol association

PHONICS SKILLS II

Initial consonant blends: sk, sl

Which ones begin with sk? Color them yellow.
Which ones begin with sl? Color them red.

Skills: Understanding that some consonant sounds can be blended together; Sound/symbol association

PHONICS SKILLS II

Initial consonant blends: sp, st

sp

st

Which ones begin with sp? Color them yellow.
Which ones begin with st? Color them orange.

PHONICS SKILLS II

Initial consonant blends: fl, fr

Print the letters and words.

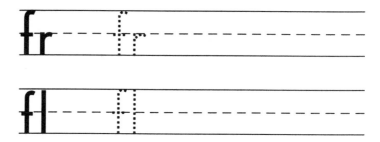

fr   fr

fl   fl

flame   flame

frame   frame

Finish the picture. Finish the word.

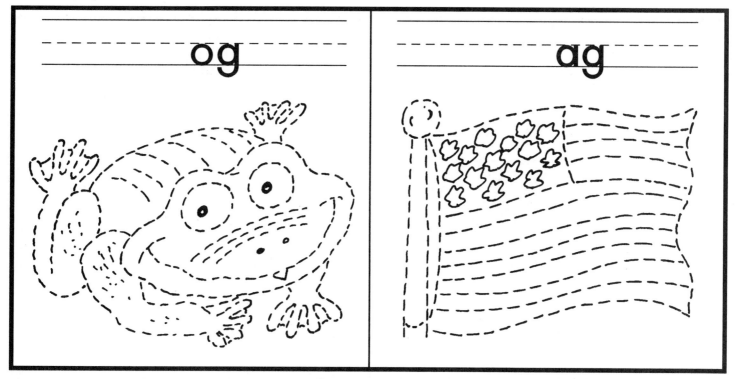

og

ag

Skills: Understanding that some consonant sounds can be blended togeher; Sound/symbol association

311

PHONICS SKILLS II

Initial consonant blends: gl, gr

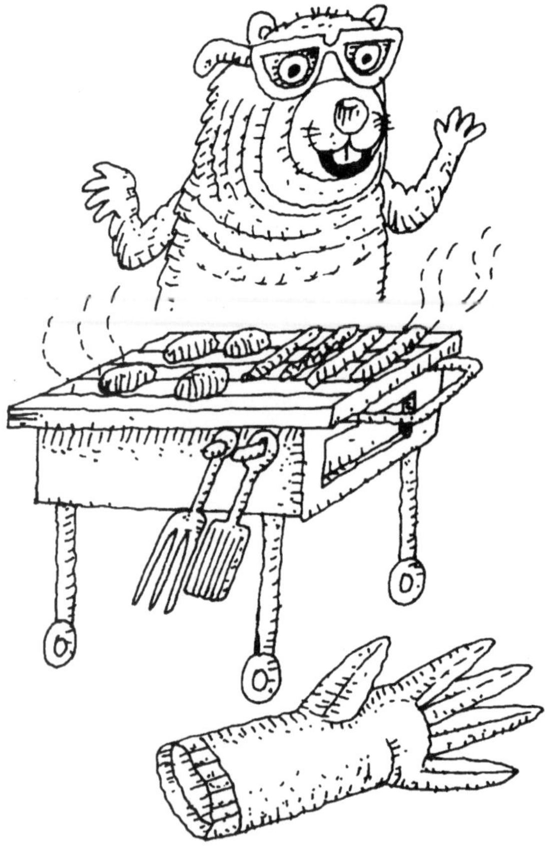

Print the letters and words.

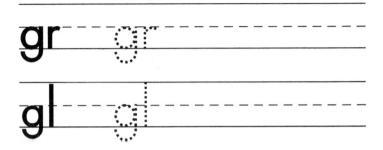

gr gr

gl gl

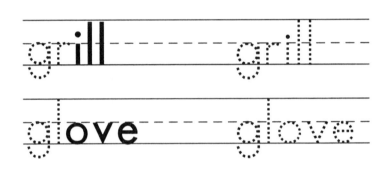

grill grill

glove glove

Finish the picture. Finish the word.

obe

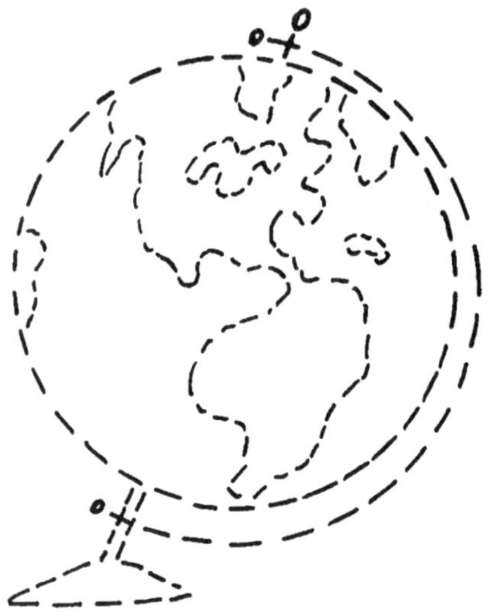

apes

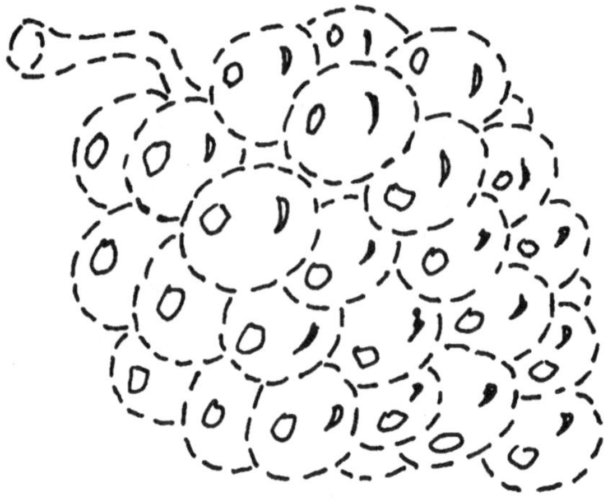

Skills: Understanding that some consonant sounds can be blended togeher; Sound/symbol association

PHONICS SKILLS II

Initial consonant blends: pl, pr

Print the letters and words.

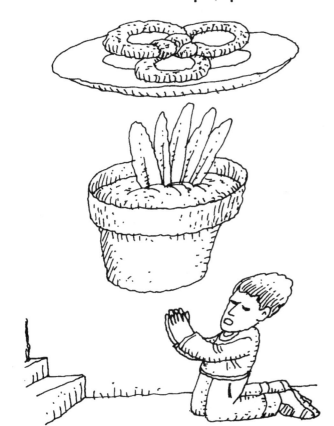

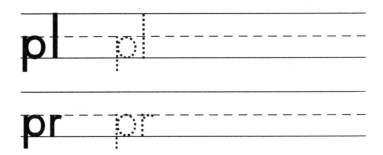

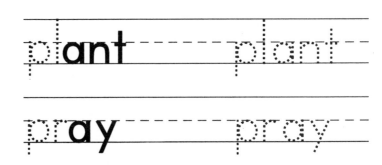

pl   pl

pr   pr

plant   plant

pray   pray

Finish the picture. Finish the word.

iers

une

Skills: Understanding that some consonant sounds can be blended togeher; Sound/symbol association

PHONICS SKILLS II

Initial consonant blends: sn, sw

Print the letters and words.

sn   sn

sw   sw

snore   snore

swan   swan

Finish the picture. Finish the word.

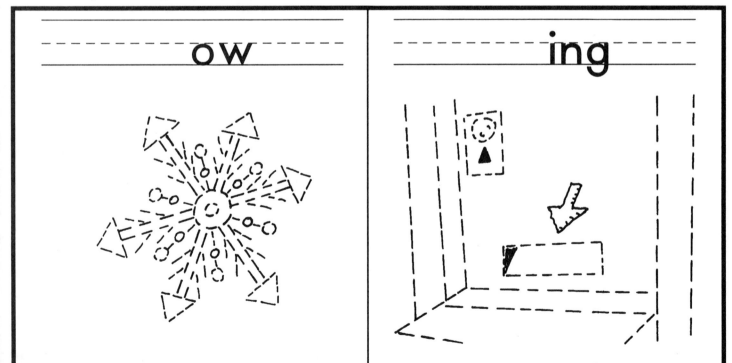

ow

ing

Skills: Understanding that some consonant sounds can be blended togeher; Sound/symbol association

PHONICS SKILLS II

Initial consonant blends: pl, pr

Print the letters and words.

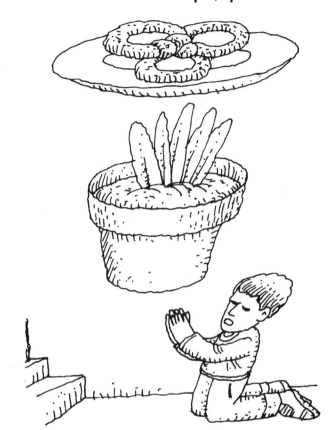

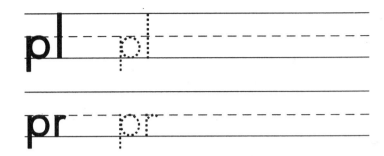

pl   pl

pr   pr

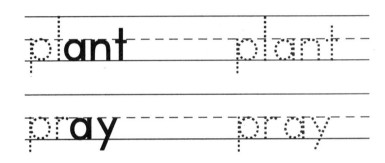

plant   plant

pray   pray

Finish the picture. Finish the word.

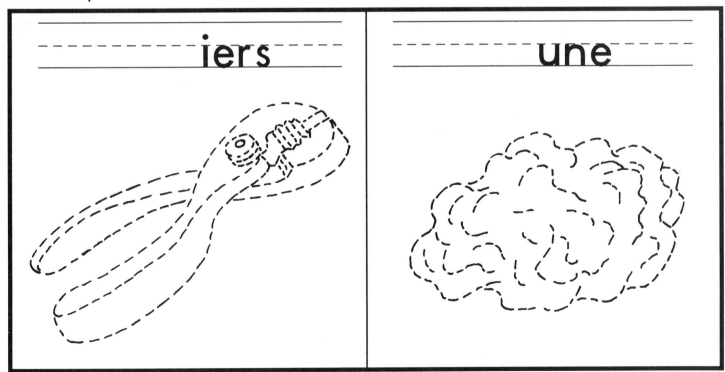

iers

une

Skills: Understanding that some consonant sounds can be blended togeher; Sound/symbol association

PHONICS SKILLS II

Initial consonant blends: sn, sw

Print the letters and words.

sn   sn

sw   sw

snore   snore

swan   swan

Finish the picture. Finish the word.

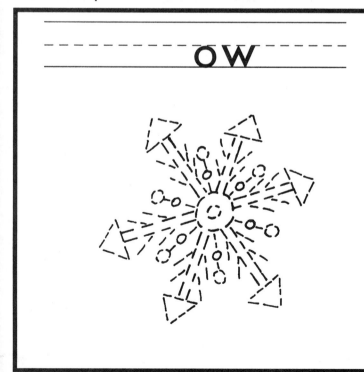

ow

ing

Skills: Understanding that some consonant sounds can be blended togeher; Sound/symbol association

314

PHONICS SKILLS II

Initial consonant blends: c r , f r , p r , t r

cr   fr   pr   tr

Say the name of each picture. Circle the two letters you hear at the beginning.
Then print the letters.

cr cl tr	cr tr fr	fr fl pr
fl fr cr	ch th fr	cr th wh
pl tr pr	cl cr tr	cl tr pr

Skills: Recognition of consonant blends; Writing letters; Auditory and visual discrimination; Writing letters

PHONICS SKILLS II

Consonant digraph: ch

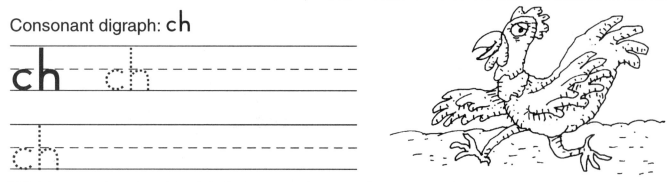

ch   ch

ch

Which ones begin with ch? Color them brown. Color the other pictures red.

Skills: Recognizing and understanding consonant digraphs; Sound/symbol association

PHONICS SKILLS II

Consonant digraph: sh

sh   sh

sh

Which ones begin with sh? Color them orange. Color the other pictures green.

Skills: Recognizing and understanding consonant digraphs; Sound/symbol association

PHONICS SKILLS II

Consonant digraph: th

th — th

th

Which ones begin with th? Color them blue. Color the other pictures red.

Skills: Recognizing and understanding consonant digraphs; Sound/symbol association

Consonant digraph: wh

wh wh

wh

Which ones begin with wh? Color them yellow. Color the other pictures blue.

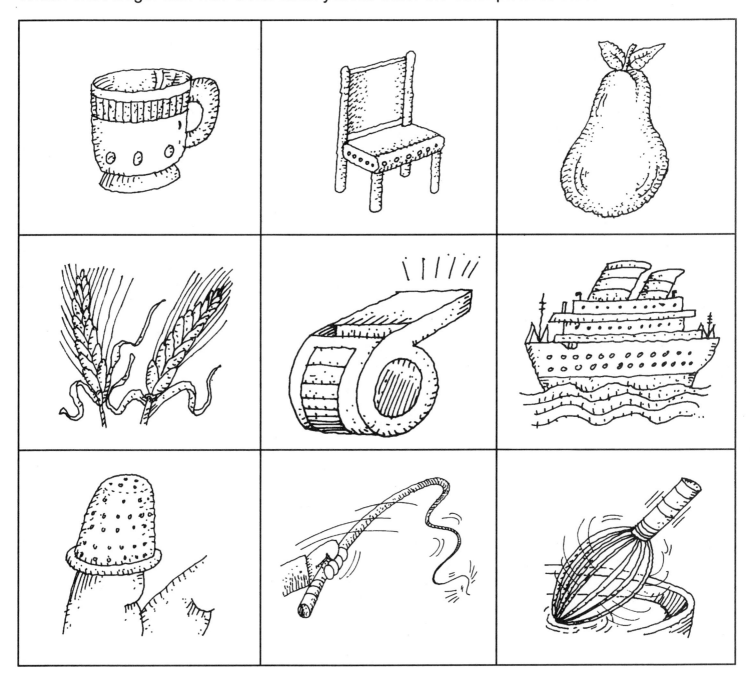

Skills: Recognizing and understanding consonant digraphs; Sound/symbol association

PHONICS SKILLS II

Consonant digraphs: c h , s h , t h , w h

ch   sh   th   wh

Say the name of each picture. Circle the two letters you hear at the beginning.
Then print the letters.

sh th th wh	ch sh th	ch sh wh	ch th wh
ch sh wh	sh ch wh	sh th wh	sh th wh
sh th wh	ch sh wh	ch th wh	ch sh th
sh th wh	sh ch wh	ch sh th	ch sh wh